How to contact your
Angels

How to contact your
Angels

Karen Paolino

David and Charles

A DAVID & CHARLES BOOK
Copyright © David & Charles Limited 2011

David & Charles is an F+W Media Inc. company
4700 East Galbraith Road
Cincinnati, OH 45236

First published in the UK in 2011

Text copyright © F+W Media Inc. 2011

The material in this book has been previously published in *The Everything Guide To Angels*, published by Adams Media, 2009.

F+W Media Inc. has asserted the right to be identified as author of this work in accordance with the Copyright, Designs and Patents Act, 1988.

A catalogue record for this book is available from the British Library.

ISBN-13: 978-1-4463-0051-0 paperback
ISBN-10: 1-4463-0051-X paperback

Printed in Finland by Bookwell
for David & Charles
Brunel House, Newton Abbot, Devon

Senior Acquisitions Editor: Freya Dangerfield
Project Editor: Felicity Barr
Art Editor: Charly Bailey
Senior Production Controller: Kelly Smith

David & Charles publish high quality books on a wide range of subjects.
For more great book ideas visit: www.rubooks.co.uk

Contents

FOREWORD

The world around you is constantly changing. Through mass media and the Internet you have a conscious awareness of how humanity is challenged every day. Because of this, people are nervous and confused and they are searching for answers. Intuitively many find themselves on the spiritual path trying to find the answers and the support they need. This is exactly why the angels are more present than ever before. They want you to feel more peaceful and they are honoured to help you in any way they can. Their mission is to help you discover the answers you seek.

The angels have different roles and assignments to help you in every possible way you can imagine. We possess the gift of free will and free choice and this is a very important point to remember when working with the angels. Because of free will, you need to ask the angels for their help and guidance. Once you ask, the angels get to work behind the scenes and you begin to witness miracles unfolding in your life.

This book is true to its title; you are going to learn everything you need to know about the angels and how to work with them. You will communicate with the angels and they will respond, with peace, clarity, encouragement, and wisdom. There is no previous experience required and you don't have to be "gifted" or psychic to communicate with the angels. They will hold your hand every step of the way. They know you better than you know yourself and

☆ ☆ ☆ ☆ ☆ ☆ ☆ ☆ ☆ ☆ ☆ ☆ ☆ ☆ ☆

they know exactly how to help you. Just be curious and open your heart to receive. You will begin to experience more joy, happiness, and peace in every aspect of your life: your relationships, your home, your career, your finances, and overall well being.

It's time to wake up and lift the veil between heaven and earth. Just remember these two truths as you embark on the journey: One, you are never alone; and two, you are always loved unconditionally by the angels.

ACKNOWLEDGMENTS

A special thank you to my earth angels, Louie, Joelle, and Justin for your loving support and encouragement. Rita, thank you for believing in me and sending me this amazing opportunity to write this book. Dottie, I am very grateful for your expertise in editing and your encouraging words every step of the way. Thank you, Lisa at Adams Media, for your guidance and your support throughout this entire process.

I am grateful to all my students and clients. By sharing their experiences with me, they taught me what's truly possible when you invite the angels into your life. Last but not least, thank you, angels, for all the blessings you've brought into my life, including this incredible opportunity to write this book. Now, others can be touched by your unconditional love and support.

An Introduction to Angels

What Are Angels?

*A*ngels are messengers that can act as the link through which you can communicate between heaven and earth. Their role is to watch over you, protect you, and guide you along your human journey. The word "angel" comes from Greek word *angelos*, which means "messenger." Angels are divine celestial beings who have not experienced living in a human body on the earth plane. They are here to serve and help humanity with compassion, grace, joy, playfulness, and peace.

Throughout history, in almost every culture and religion, there have been stories and validations of the angels and their roles as messengers from heaven to earth. Their presence is portrayed in many different forms. In different religious scripture such as the Bible, the Koran, and the Kabbalah, the angels have been described as healers, messengers, and guides. Artists throughout time have been inspired by angels. Their paintings depict angels in various forms—a glowing light and aura surrounding them, human-like beings with glorious wings, some with a halo above their head or a musical instrument in their hands. Their appearance and purpose may vary throughout the world and its history, but their universal influence over mankind is a presence of love, guidance, and a reminder that we are not alone.

One important reminder: You were given two gifts to experience in this lifetime: free will and free choice. Whatever choices you make and however those choices play out, the angels are there to watch over in unconditional love. One important point about this gift of free will is that the angels will not interfere in your life unless you ask them. The only time they will intervene is if there is a life-threatening situation and it's not your time to leave this earth plane. This is called divine intervention, and they will do whatever it takes to save your life. So the most important thing to remember when working with these divine celestial beings is to ask for help and guidance when you need it. This opens the doors to invite miracles into your life and to receive clear communication from the angels.

How Many Angels Are There?

There is a great curiosity about how many angels there are. Scripture does not quote the exact numbers, but it does allude to their massive presence. Everyone has at least two guardian angels assigned to them, and they will be with you from birth to the time of death. So to get an idea about how many guardian angels there are think about the number of human beings that have existed throughout time and multiply that number by two. Add that number to the divine helpers from the hierarchy of angels and other ministering angels who have their individual roles in the divine order.

What Do Angels Look Like?

This is a very important question for those seeking to know more about the angels and how to connect with them. Angels have been portrayed in many forms: with wings and without, male and female, human and child, with a sword or trumpet, radiating in pure light or even appearing in multiple colours of light. This opens discussion to the possibility that everyone may have a different perception of angels. Many interpretations of the angels and what they look like are based on a person's viewpoint, their culture, religious upbringing, belief system, and even their strongest intuitive senses.

As you seek your own path of spiritual growth and intuition development, you will learn to trust your own experience of the angels and what they look or feel like to you. The angels know you better than you know yourself; be reassured that if you ask them, they will make their presence known to you.

Who Sees the Angels?

The angels are all around you and they appear in many forms. A veil separates you from the ability to see heaven and earth as one. For children, the veil is thinner and their beliefs are not clouded with fear, so many of them can naturally see the angels. Sometimes parents will witness their children interacting with "imaginary friends." This could very possibly be their guardian angels communicating and playing with them.

When close to the moment of death, some patients have reported witnessing an apparition of an angel or loved one coming to escort them back home. Those who are grieving from the loss of a loved one are also more open to receiving a visitation from the angels. One way the angels can appear to them is during their dream state. Many who have had this experience share that it seemed so real, even though they knew it was a dream.

☆ ☆ ☆ ☆ ☆ ☆ ☆ ☆ ☆ ☆ ☆ ☆ ☆ ☆ ☆

Have you ever seen flashes or sparkles of light around you? Or have you ever seen a shadow of someone or something out of the corner of your eye? These can be a manifestation of the angels' presence around you. Who can see the angels? Anyone can open their awareness to see the angels. It takes an open mind and heart and a desire to see beyond the veil.

Are Our Loved Ones Angels?

Many people feel and experience their loved ones who have passed as their guardian angels. Their presence and love never leaves you and, yes, it can feel as if they are still around you acting as your guardian angel. As mentioned before, the angels have never been in a physical form. They are celestial beings of pure light, love, and energy.

Angel Advice

Mediums

You need to invest wisely and choose someone with experience and expertise. You can also look for a Spiritualist Church in your area. This is a spiritual community where the congregation gathers for healing and experienced mediums bring messages through from spirits.

Those that have passed and are now living in the spirit world are better referred to as spirit guides. Some loved ones may choose as part of their soul plan and evolution to be a spirit to help you along your life's journey. It is said that those relatives you were named after at the time of birth have a soul contract to watch over you as spirit guides after their transition to the other side. If you feel a loss or miss a loved one who is not with you anymore, open the channels of communication with them just like you would contact the angels. They are still with you in spirit and if you choose to, you can attune to their ever-present love and guidance.

If you are interested in communicating with your loved ones in spirit, do your research and seek out an experienced medium. They have natural abilities or they have developed their skills to communicate with this world. Their job is to deliver evidential information and messages of love proving the continuity of life after death. This information can be very healing and it can bring peace to those who are missing their loved ones.

How Can the Angels Help You?

Legions of angels are all around you and wait in assistance to serve you in countless ways. Angels are here to help with healing of all kinds—physical, emotional, and even healing of relationships and pets. If it's physical or emotional healing you need, they will surround you with loving, healing energy and empower you to connect with your own inner healer. If you need outside support from others, they will connect you with the right people or resources you need to help you achieve health and wholeness. If you are in pain they will provide comfort and peace to help ease the pain.

If there is need for healing in your relationships with others, you can call on the angels for help. They may ask you to practice forgiveness, they may encourage you to communicate and express your feelings, or they can even give you peace if you need to let go of the relationship that is causing you pain.

Ask the Angel

How do I ask the angels for help?

There is no formal way to ask. You can simply call out to the angels by name or you can say, "Angels, gather around me and surround me in your love." Then ask for whatever you need. No prayer is too small or too large. Surrender your prayer to divine resolution and trust that your prayer has been heard and will be answered in divine timing.

If you are seeking a soul mate or looking for new friends, ask the angels for divine intervention so you connect with each other at the perfect place and time. If it's time to look for a new place to live or buy a car, make a wish list of what you want. Give it to the angels, then pay attention and expect miracles. If you want help finding a new job or you need courage to live your life purpose, know the angels will be honored to assist you in any way they can. There are also angels who act as financial advisers in spirit.

They can assist you in finding resources or opportunities to increase your income and can help you heal debt and create financial balance.

Do You Need to be "Gifted" to Connect with the Angels?

You don't have to be special or gifted to connect with the angels and receive messages of divine guidance. It simply requires an open mind and heart; and a desire to learn.

Through the eyes of the angels there is no one more special than the other. It is a choice, and everyone has the ability to connect with the angels. It takes curiosity and a willingness to expand your consciousness beyond what you can see and touch. Choose to travel down the path of spiritual growth. Be open and willing to learn all you can. Learn to meditate, open your *chakras* (energy centres that run throughout the body), and attune your senses to the oneness of energy all around you.

Be Open to Angels

It's very natural to be a skeptic before a believer. Be a student and a curious seeker on the path of spirituality. Remember, the angels work only in the vibration of love, and this is their pure intention. If you experience fear, it resonates within you. This fear may come from a variety of sources: your parents' beliefs, what you were taught in school, society, religion, television, and possibly fears from past life experiences. No matter what the source may be, you can change your belief system and decide what's true for you.

Your truth will unfold with experience. As you open up to the angels, pay attention to your feelings and only do what feels right to you. The angels want you to feel safe and protected. They will walk side by side with you as you learn and grow.

When you invite the angels into your life, expect positive changes to occur. One of the greatest gifts you will receive is knowing that you are never alone. The fear of being alone is a deep, unconscious fear that many deal with. When the angels are a part of your life this fear no longer exists. As you give your prayers and requests to the angels you begin to trust you have a team working behind the scenes. You experience a sense of peace and relief that you are not alone in your worries. Life becomes exciting, and you look forward to playing with the angels every day.

The angels see you and your life experiences through the eyes of unconditional love. You are never judged for your choices or actions. There is nothing you could ever have said or done that would compromise the angels' love for you. If you learn to accept their love it will be easier for you to love yourself, and when you love yourself it is easier to love another.

CONNECT WITH THE ANGELS: RAISE YOUR VIBRATIONS AND ATTUNE YOUR ENERGY

Energy and Vibration

*I*t's important to understand the concept of energy and vibration so you can experience the angels with all your senses. You are energy and the angels are energy. If this is true, then why can't you see the angels like you can see other human beings? It has to do with the concept of vibration. The meaning of vibration from the *Merriam-Webster Dictionary* is, "a characteristic emanation, aura, or spirit that infuses or vitalises someone or something and that can be instinctively sensed or experienced." Here is the key: In order to see or feel the energy of the angels, you need to raise your vibration to be in tune with their energy. The angels vibrate in the energy of pure divine love and humans resonate between the energy of fear and love.

Angel Advice

If you're ever having a bad day and want to feel better, simply smile. Fake it if you need to. Try it right now; smile and see how you feel. Notice how your energy changes. This is a simple technique to raise your vibration. You can change any situation, no matter where you are or who you are with, by just smiling.

The energy of fear resonates at a lower vibration, while the energy of love resonates at a higher vibration. Think about the last time you were around someone who was angry, depressed, or confused. What "vibe" did you get from that person? Did they lift you up or bring you down? Now think of an occasion when you were with someone who was fun, who made you laugh, and you had a really good time. What vibe did you get from this person? Did their energy lift your spirits or bring you down?

If you would like to hear, feel, and see the angels, you need to raise your vibration to become one with their energy. The following are ways to raise your vibration, but the keys are patience and practice. Discover which ones feel comfortable to you and your lifestyle. It's important to find a method that you enjoy and you feel connected to. When this happens, you are more likely to stick with it and use it to bond with the angels.

Silence

When sitting in stillness and silence, the mind and the body relax. By becoming still you can seek to find your center, where the ego mind quiets and the gateway to the divine opens. The angels want to get your attention and communicate with you, and it's easier when you can find this place to connect.

Silence is the pathway to follow on your journey to the center of the self. In this silence you begin to experience a unity and you recognise you are one with the divine.

☆ ☆ ☆ ☆ ☆ ☆ ☆ ☆ ☆ ☆ ☆ ☆ ☆ ☆ ☆

Angel Advice

In order to experience the presence of angels, you must dare to turn off the electronic sounds around you. In order to come to your spiritual center, listen instead to the simpler sounds around you. You might hear a bird chirping, rain dripping, or the simple sound of your own breath or perhaps the flutter of an angel's wings or an angel singing.

Silence is a great spiritual teacher who guides you and illuminates your way when it is dark. In the silence of the inner self, you reach truth, and in so doing, you find your angels there, guiding and gracing you and delivering the messages you need to hear. The angels want to help you and they want you to be able to recognise their presence in your life.

Fortunately, you do not have to retire to a monastery or become a hermit to experience the contemplative silence that is at the heart of experiencing the angelic world. You can achieve your own silence and recognise the presence of angels by practicing silence on a daily basis.

Guided Meditation

Some people have a difficult time sitting in silence because their mind is too busy. If this sounds familiar to you, then try guided meditation. In guided meditation you listen to the voice of

☆ ☆ ☆ ☆ ☆ ☆ ☆ ☆ ☆ ☆ ☆ ☆ ☆ ☆ ☆

someone who guides you through the process of meditation.

Most guided meditations combine soothing music with the use of visualisation. Both techniques are used to help you relax and to enhance the experience. Your thoughts are focused on following the direction of the guide and it's easier to let go as you allow your experiences to unfold.

Most guided mediations start with a deep relaxation of the body and the mind. After you slow down your breath and release the tension in your body, you will physically and mentally relax. When this happens you naturally open up the pathway to other states of consciousness. In this altered state you can enhance your spiritual growth and development and you can communicate with the angels. Ask the angels to work with you in meditation to help you better understand who they are and how they can help you.

Angel Advice

There are many forms of meditation. It's best to experiment with different types of meditation to discover what works best for you. If you have a hard time quieting your mind or if you are just getting started, you might want to seek out a meditation class in your area or purchase a guided meditation CD.

☆ ☆ ☆ ☆ ☆ ☆ ☆ ☆ ☆ ☆ ☆ ☆ ☆ ☆ ☆

The following guided meditation will help you raise your vibration so you can attune to the angels and receive their loving guidance. During this attunement you can release your fears and ask the angels for the help you need. They will work with you during the attunement, and they will help you raise your vibration so you can feel them, hear them, and possibly see them.

It would be helpful if you could record the words beforehand so you can simply relax and listen during meditation. Remember to speak slowly and with a soothing voice when you record the meditation. Try playing soothing music in the background during your recording.

Take some nice deep breaths and just close your eyes. Set the intention with your angels to attune to their energy and raise your vibration so you can easily see, feel, hear, and sense their loving presence. (Pause)

Now ask the angels to surround you in a beautiful circle of divine light, love, and protection. Take a moment and breathe with them and feel their unconditional love flow into every cell of your being. As you do this, your body begins to relax. Feel this soothing and healing divine light flow into the top of your head, relaxing your scalp; all the muscles in your scalp relax. Now, feel it flow into your forehead and then your eyes, cheeks, jaw, and your mouth. All the muscles in your face relax. (Pause) Feel the light and relaxation flow into your neck, relaxing your neck. Feel it flow into your shoulders, down your arms, and to the tips of your fingers. It feels so good to relax and let go. (Pause) Now, breathe in the divine light into your chest and feel all your muscles relax in your chest. Then feel it flow into your stomach and all the muscles in your stomach relax. (Pause) Now, bring awareness to your back, and feel the divine light flow down your back relaxing your upper back, your middle back, all the way down to your lower back. Your entire back relaxes in this beautiful soothing light. (Pause) Feel as the light and relaxation flows down into your hips, your knees, your calves, and all the way down to the soles of your feet, the tips of your toes. (Pause) Your entire body is filled with relaxation and the divine light. Every cell of your being is illuminated with this divine light. Notice how good it feels to relax and let go. (Pause)

Imagine the angels give you this beautiful cloud chair and they ask you to sit in it and relax. This cloud chair was made just for you and it fits you perfectly. You melt into the cloud chair and relax even deeper. (Pause) Feel and imagine 10,000 angels surrounding you. Welcome them, breathe with them, and know they are there to help you. (Pause) They slowly begin to lift your cloud chair into the higher octaves of the angelic realm. Imagine your cloud chair being carried upward into the higher vibration of the angelic realm where only love exists. They know exactly what they are doing, so just trust and allow them to attune your energy to this higher vibration of love and light. (Pause) As you relax and attune to the higher vibrations of light, notice what you feel, what you hear, what you see, and what you sense. (Pause) Take a moment and release your fears to them. They have the ability to dissolve them so you can receive healing and clarity. (Pause) Now, share with them your prayers and desires. Ask for the help you need. (Pause) Trust that your prayers have been heard and they will be answered.

This attunement has transformed you. From this moment forward, you will be more in tune with the angels that surround you. You will sense their energy around you. You will hear more clearly their messages of divine guidance. You will understand how they are trying to get your attention. Know that because of this attunement, you will experience more joy, peace, fulfillment, and happiness in your life. You deserve it and the angels are there to help you create it. Just remember to ask for their help when you need it. You are never, ever alone, and you are loved unconditionally by God and the angels.

Take a moment and thank the angels. (Pause) Ask that they continue to guide you in every way.

Now feel or imagine as they bring your cloud chair slowly back into the present moment. Take some nice deep breaths and feel as you ground yourself in the moment of now. Feel light, free, and grateful, and filled with light and love. (Pause) Expect peace. Expect miracles. Expect better than you could ever imagine.

Use this guided meditation whenever you desire relaxation or if you want to let go and ask the angels for help and guidance. They are always there for you and guided meditation can be a powerful tool to help you make that connection.

Working with the Breath

Angels are pure spirit, and you can raise your vibration and enhance your connection to their world simply by using breath techniques (breath is synonymous with spirit). By becoming aware of your breathing, you become aware of your spiritual nature, for breath is life. Thus, you can use your breath, as a yogi does, to elevate your consciousness to the realm where the angels dwell. In other words, the breath is the gateway to the sacred angelic dimension.

The breath is something you take for granted. Without the breath there is no life. Most times you are unaware of the breath until you experience a shortness of breath or panic sets in and your breath speeds up. When you become aware of your breathing you connect to your spiritual self.

When you enhance the breath and use it to open up to different realms, your natural abilities begin to unfold—mental, physical, emotional, and spiritual. It unblocks energy and channels of communication open up; information can flow into your consciousness. Conscious breathing develops a communications link between body and mind, between conscious and unconscious, between spirit and angels.

Here is a rhythmic breathing technique that you can use at any time to raise your vibration. You can do it almost anywhere, whether sitting quietly at home, in your car, or when walking. It's simple and it can help you connect with your inner power.

Relax and close your eyes. Observe your breath pattern, but do not make any attempt to alter it. Just pay attention to the breath going in and coming out. Now, begin to breathe slowly and deeply. Feel the warmth of used air leave your body and breathe in fresh clean air. Imagine yourself being cleansed and energized by each breath.

Now listen to any sounds you make while breathing. Don't judge it, just listen. Also notice whether you breathe in shallow or deep breaths and where the air goes—into the diaphragm or the belly. Does your chest rise or fall or does your abdomen rise or fall?

As you inhale and exhale—allow the breath to become one continuous movement (with no separation or gaps between the inhale and the exhale). Continue doing this for several minutes and notice how you feel.

Affirmations

Another way to raise your vibration is to empower yourself by changing your thoughts from negative to positive. You can do this by writing or saying an affirmation. An affirmation is declaring the truth through a positive statement. For example, if you are continuously saying, "There must not be angels because I cannot see or feel them," change that statement and affirm, "I know there are plenty of angels here for me. I am willing to see and feel their loving presence." If your thoughts are filled with fear and doubt you will continue to experience the same. As you think, so shall you be. You need to fake it until you make it through the power of affirmations. When you practice using affirmations, you shift your thoughts to experience what you want versus what you don't want.

Chanting

Chanting is an ancient ritual, and it's been used in different religious and ritual ceremonies to access the divine. Through the power of chanting you can reach altered states of consciousness and raise your vibration to connect with the divine. Chanting can transform negative energy into positive energy, which immediately raises your vibration. When you chant certain phrases over and over again, it shifts the vibration and causes change in mind, body, and spirit. You quiet the mind, you open the heart, and you lift your spirit to a higher state of consciousness.

There are no hard-set rules for chanting. You can chant anywhere—in the shower, at work, in the car, or while you're walking outdoors.

Here are some different forms of chanting you can check into and practice:

✫ The OM chant is a universally recognized chant. Take in a breath and on the out breath, draw out the sound of OM like this: "oooooommmmmmmmmmm," putting the emphasis on the last part.

✫ Gregorian chanting is a beautiful form of music and chanting. You can buy Gregorian chanting CDs online. Play them during meditation or listen to them in the car. You can also seek out a local church that sings this medieval form of music.

✫ Use a mala, a string of beads used to count mantras or Sanskrit prayers. A mantra can be a word or series of words chanted out loud. As you touch each bead, repeat your mantra. You can use a Sanskrit mantra meaning peace—"Shanti,

Shanti, Shanti," or you can repeat English words like "I am" or "love."

★ Use rosary beads and say one of the following prayers: Our Father Hail Mary, or Glory Be.

The most important thing about chanting is finding the method that feels right for you. Experiment and see what form of chanting creates a connection between you and the divine. When you make that connection, you will feel it in every cell of your being.

Release Fear and Remember Love

Fear can clog your energy centers or chakras. It lowers your vibration and blocks the flow of divine guidance. It's important to become conscious of when you are focusing on fear. Choose to recognise it, stop it, and focus on the positive. Fear comes in many forms: worry, stress, confusion, anger, and the list goes on. Feel the low vibration of these energies and imagine how it can weigh you down. In each and every moment, you can make a choice to let go of fear and focus your thoughts on faith. Ask the angels to lift your fears and help you remember your choices based on love.

Gratitude

To be grateful is to recognise the blessings in your life. Gratitude is a wonderful way to open up the energy of your heart chakra. Each and every time you have thoughts of gratitude or you express gratitude, you raise your vibration and heighten your awareness to recognise the miracles all around you.

Angel Advice

A way to practice gratitude is to buy a journal you love and either start your day or end your day by writing ten things you are grateful for. It is so simple and it can transform your life. If you choose, you can multiply the blessings in your life and open your awareness to experience the graces of the angels all around you.

Practice recognising the small things in life you are grateful for: a thank you or a smile from a stranger, a good cup of coffee, a sunny day, or finding time to read a good book. To raise your vibration during difficult times, choose to focus on the blessings in your life. For example, if you are going through financial difficulties, be grateful for having the money to pay the essentials, food and shelter. If you are challenged with a physical illness, be grateful for those that are there to help you in your time of need. If you are grieving a loss or separation with a family member or close friend, focus on the love and support from those that are still in your life. You have the power and the choice to change any situation in your life. Choose to start today and focus on the positive, focus on the love in your life, and expect life to change for the better.

Opening up to the Angels

What Drew You to This Book?

*A*s you journey down the path of spiritual growth you realise that nothing happens by mistake and everything happens for a reason. This book is in your hands because it was meant to be. The angels want to work with you, this is an exciting time. Open your heart, open your mind, and be curious as you open up to the possibilities of experiencing heaven on earth.

Belief

Believing something to be possible opens the door to experience. So are you ready to take your first step? Invite the angels into your life and choose to believe in their existence. Ask them to plant a seed of faith into your heart so you can trust and believe the angels are there for you in unconditional love. Take a moment and breathe with the angels and ask them to help you believe.

Angel Prayer

Here's a prayer you can say to the angels: "Dearest angels, please help me believe in your presence and show me that you are there for me in all ways, always. Help me believe that anything is possible when you have faith and trust in God and the angels. Thank you."

To enhance your belief in the angels, read more about them, learn all that you can, and surround yourself with others who believe. As you expand your awareness to the possibilities that exist, you increase your opportunities to experience it for yourself. Trust that the angels want you to believe in them so they can make your life better.

Believing in the angels requires patience. You want certain things to happen now and sometimes it's just a matter of time. During these restless moments, pray for patience, keep the faith, and believe the angels are working behind the scenes. Ask the angels to empower you with patience and perseverance and trust that your desire is coming to fruition.

Learning Opens Awareness

Learning something new provides you with the opportunity to experience something different. This is especially important when opening up to the angels. The angels' world is not tangible; you cannot touch it and you cannot see it with the human eye. Therefore, you must expand your awareness to think outside of the box.

If you want to increase your intuitive abilities so you can communicate with the angelic realm, study and learn as much as you can. Your desire and motivation creates the energy of enthusiasm that is like a magnet, drawing to you everything that you need to develop your skills.

It's important to understand that the angels communicate with you through your database of information and knowledge. So as you expand your knowledge and you enhance your intuition, they have more ways to communicate with you. For example, if the angels see that you are paying attention to coincidences and synchronicities, then they will use this method of communication to get your attention.

Desire

Your focused desire to create a deeper connection with the angels will make things happen. Start by having a heart-to-heart dialog with your angels to open the lines of communication. Talk to the angels as if you were talking to your best friend and share with them your deepest desires and wishes. Remember, they already know who you are and everything there is to know about you. They are excited to make the connection with you and to help you in any way they can.

One way you can do this is to write a letter to the angels. Put your desires on paper and share with them why you are ready to connect with them at this time. Speak from your heart. Share your fears, worries, and concerns and ask them to help you manifest your true desires.

Take some quiet time for yourself and find a peaceful place to sit. You can start your letter by saying, "Dearest angels" . . . and then allow your thoughts to flow on to paper. Try not to think, just write. When you're finished, put your letter away and release your desires to the angels with love. Say thank you in advance for all the help and guidance coming your way. The angels stand by your side waiting for you to ask for their help. As you give them your desires they become your team in spirit, working behind the scenes to make things happen.

The Power of Intention

After you share your desires and wishes with the angels, take another step and get clear about your intentions. An intention declares your determination and effort to obtain a goal. When you state your intentions to the angels you set a powerful energy into motion. Your intentions are an invisible force of energy that makes things happen. Get clear about what you want and the rewards will be well worth the effort.

Remember, when working with the law of free will and free choice, you need to ask the angels for help. Get clear about what you want and why you need help. Then express or write your intentions and ask the angels for help. When you claim your intentions and put them into action, you ignite the divine power within you to make things happen. Imagine what the results can be when you combine your power with the team of angels waiting to assist you. Miracles happen, and you realise the possibilities are endless as you open up to help, guidance, and clear communication with the angels.

Here are some examples of stating your intentions:

* Help me release my fears that block clear communication with the angels.
* Heal my wounds from any past experiences that may block clear communication with the angels.

☆ ☆ ☆ ☆ ☆ ☆ ☆ ☆ ☆ ☆ ☆ ☆ ☆ ☆ ☆

✫ Build my faith and trust so I can believe in angels.
✫ Help me hear, see, and feel your presence around me.
✫ Help me notice the ways in which the angels are trying to get my attention to answer my prayers.
✫ Show me the books and guide me to the people that will help me communicate with the angels.

Notice which intentions feel right for you and declare them to your angels. You can repeat them in your thoughts, you can write them down on paper, or you can speak them out loud. The way you choose to express your intentions each carries a different vibration of energy. Notice what the energy feels like when you repeat your intentions in your thoughts. Then feel the energy increase when you write them. Then feel the energy expand once again when you say them out loud. The more energy you put into your intentions the more powerful they become.

Focus on What You Want

You are a powerful person and you can manifest what you desire with the help of the angels. It's important to take responsibility and own your individual power. One way you can do this is to choose your thoughts and words wisely. Have you ever heard the saying, "As you think, so shall you be"? Your thoughts and words influence what you experience in your life. To clarify this, imagine you are surrounded by a magnetic field. Your words and thoughts become the magnetic force that attracts to you what you experience in your everyday life. To phrase it another way, your life becomes a mirror reflection of your thoughts.

There is a key factor to remember as you become this powerful magnetic attraction. Be clear with your intentions and focus on what you want, not what you don't want. The universe does not know the difference between your wants and your don't wants, it just magnetizes to you what you are focused on.

If you ask for what you want to happen but your thoughts and words are focused on what you don't want, you are sending out a mixed message to the universe. For example, if your intention is, "Help me hear, see, and feel the presence of the angels around me" but your thoughts and words are focused on, "I can't see anything. I don't feel anything," you are counteracting your intention and blocking your ability to receive what you want.

Just by changing your thoughts and words, the magic unfolds and what seemed impossible becomes possible .The following are examples of how you can transform and redirect your intention to create what you desire.

Don't Want	Do Want
"I don't know what to believe"	"I believe in angels and miracles"
"I am not good enough"	"I am good enough. I deserve the best"
"I don't have time to meditate"	"I listen to my angels in the shower and in the car"
"My prayers are not being answered"	"My prayers are answered in divine time"

Surrender to the Angels

Once you have asked the angels for help you need to trust and surrender your prayer to them. This can be hard for some people who have a hard time letting go of control. If this applies to you, contemplate this thought: Do you trust that the angels have your best interest in mind? If so, it's time to surrender.

A wonderful way to surrender is to find or create a surrender box. Place all your desires, wishes, and intentions into this box and then affirm, "I am letting go. I am open to my highest and best, better than I could ever imagine." By doing this ritual, you release it from your control and you give it to the angels for miracles to occur. You break free from your human limited thinking and you open up to the unlimited possibilities of divine resolution to occur. Once you surrender, it's your job to trust. Release your expectations and trust that everything is in divine order.

A Meditation to Reconnect with the Divine

Find a quiet place to sit where you will not be disturbed. You can do this meditation in silence or play soft meditative music in the background.

Get as comfortable as you can and take a deep breath and close your eyes.

Take another deep breath and let go of everything that happened before you closed your eyes.

Take another deep breath and let go of everything that is going to happen after you open your eyes. Now breathe into the present moment and just let go.

With intention, fill the room with divine white light and energy and begin to breathe one with that divine light.

Ask your angels to surround you in a beautiful circle of love, light, and protection.

Remember you are never alone and you are very loved.

Now, imagine a beautiful spiritual sun in front of you. This sun is the energy of the divine.

To become one with this energy and divine light, imagine that you have a plug (just like a lamp has a plug to plug into electricity) coming from your solar plexus and, using your imagination, plug into the spiritual sun.

Now breathe in the energy and light from this sun into your body as if every cell in your physical body illuminates with this light.

Imagine that you can then breathe into your mind the divine wisdom and guidance you are searching for. Your mind and thoughts illuminate in this light.

You feel lighter and more peaceful with every breath that you take.

Now your body and your mind are illuminated in this light. You are no longer separate from this divine source. You are one with the angels, and all that is.

Breathe the light in, be one, feel the peace, feel the love. It is yours and it always has been. (Pause)

Before you come back, think of a question you would like answered by divine guidance. Ask the angels for divine guidance and then listen for your answer.

Say thank you. To return, just take some nice deep breaths and begin to feel your body, feel yourself back in the room.

Remember, you can plug in any time you choose. Each and every time you do, you reconnect with the divine wisdom and healing that's rightfully yours.

Developing Your Intuition with the Angels

What Is Intuition?

*I*ntuition is the instinctual knowing you get when you listen to your inner senses. Everyone is intuitive, and you can train yourself to become more attuned to your senses. Some people may be more sensitive to what they feel; their intuition speaks to them through sensations in their body. Others may be more sensitive to what they hear, and their intuition speaks to them through their inner thoughts or ideas. Seek to discover which senses you use the most and which ones stand out more distinctly. This helps you focus on your strongest senses to receive intuitive information.

Your intuition is a direct link to the angels. As you develop your intuition, your senses heighten and you learn to trust what you hear, feel, and sense from the angels. You are more intuitive than you realise. The more you can understand and listen to your intuition the better it can guide you. Below is a list of expressions that people use when they are connected to their intuition. Check and see if you use any of these phrases:

☆ I had a feeling. Have you ever had a feeling that something was going to happen and then it did? Did you ever have the feeling you needed to call someone and when you did they needed your help?

☆ Something told me. Did you ever hear an inner voice guide you, telling you what to do?

✷ I had a dream. Did you ever get a direct message from someone in a dream or did you ever have a dream that later had significant meaning?

✷ I had a gut feeling. Did you ever not trust your gut feeling and disaster followed? Now think about a time when you did follow your gut feeling and everything worked out.

✷ I just knew. Did you ever have that inner understanding and you knew you were right and nobody could change your mind?

As you pay attention to your senses and you learn to interpret their messages, your intuition can become very valuable. It can direct you to the answers you are seeking.

Try this intuitive exercise. Close your eyes and place your hand on your heart. Take a couple of nice deep breaths. Ask which friend or family member needs to receive a phone call from you. Notice how you feel when you hear that name and ask if there is anything you need to know. Then call that person and see how accurate your intuition was. Don't be surprised if that person picks up the phone and calls you first.

Direct and Indirect Intuition

Your intuition can communicate in two different ways. Direct intuition is literal and you know exactly what your intuition is saying to you. For example, you are putting an addition onto your house and you have asked the angels to help you find the perfect people to help you build it. You go to the gym and during a break you talk to one of the members. As you are talking, he mentions he's a builder looking for work. There is no interpretation to be made—this is a direct answer to your prayers.

Then there is indirect intuition, which is more symbolic, and you need to contemplate its interpretation. Let's say you are meditating and you've invited your angels into your meditation to give you guidance. You have been looking for a new space to rent for your business. You ask the angels in meditation, "Is the place I looked at today the right space for me to rent?" In your meditation your inner vision shows you a stop sign, but up ahead in the road is a green light. This is a symbolic, indirect way your intuition is communicating with you. When you ask your angels to help you interpret the vision, you realise this place for your business is not the right one (stop sign symbol) but further down the road there is a better choice coming (light is green symbol).

What Are the Clair Senses?

Communication from the angels flows through your psychic senses called "clair" senses. These correspond with the senses you use: seeing, feeling, hearing, knowing, tasting, and smelling. It's important to become familiar with these different clairs. By learning more about them you can pay attention to your senses and use them to receive clear communication from the angels.

★ *Clairvoyance* is clear vision. This is when you have visions, images, or symbols presented to you through your inner vision.

★ *Clairsentience* is clear feeling. This is when you receive information as a feeling in your body.

★ *Clairaudience* is clear hearing. This is when you experience or hear clear thoughts or words flowing through your mind and no one is physically talking to you.

★ *Claircognizance* is clear knowing. When you have an inner knowing and you feel very strongly that something is true or you know beyond any doubt that you need to take action.

★ *Clairgustance* is clear taste. When you experience this you have a clear taste of something in your mouth without any explanation of why it's happening.

★ *Clairolfactory* is clear smell. When you use this ability you can smell something even though it's not physically in your presence.

If you choose to become more intuitive or psychic, learn the different clairs and practice using them. Everyone is psychic and everyone can develop his or her abilities. The more you learn to trust the information you receive, the more you can use its valuable information in everyday life.

Clairvoyance: "Clear Seeing"

Many people want to see the angels with their physical eye, but it's easier to perceive them with your inner vision or your third eye. The third eye is located in the center of your forehead right between your eyebrows. It is the energy center where spiritual visions are transmitted and received. When your third eye is open and clear, you have the ability to receive impressions, visions, and symbols about past, present, and future events.

Angel Advice

Precognition is when you receive visions or information about a future event. Most people have precognitive dreams, but it can also happen during meditation or just walking down the street. These visions can be positive or they can be upsetting when the vision pertains to an upcoming death or disaster. If you have precognitive experiences, ask the angels to help you feel comfortable with your ability. It can be a gift, not a burden.

There are so many blessings to receive by opening your third eye and becoming clairvoyant. You can ask for answers and insight to come to you during your dream state. You can ask for clarity from the angels about relationships, health, finances, or even making a decision in order to move forward. Another blessing of being clairvoyant is seeing images of your angels through your third eye or with your physical eyes open.

The best way to receive clairvoyant insight is to put some time aside for meditation during your day. As you sit in silence, allow the visions or symbols to flow through your consciousness. You can ask the angels for guidance on a specific question and then witness what goes through your thoughts. If an image or symbol flashes across your consciousness, go back and ask the angels to clarify what it means.

Meditation for Clairvoyance: Opening Your Third Eye

Find a quiet place to sit where you will not be disturbed.

Ask the angels to surround you with divine love, light, and protection. Share with the angels your desire to become more clairvoyant and ask them to help you open your third eye so you can receive clear visions, symbols, and insight. Then surrender, allow them to help you and breathe into the divine light surrounding you. With your eyes closed, imagine a beautiful spiritual sun in front of you, the source of love, wisdom, and guidance. Breathe and become one with its light. (Pause) Remind yourself that it's your natural divine birthright to see clearly into this divine wisdom and to receive the answers you are seeking.

Now, bring awareness to your third eye in the middle of your forehead. Imagine that you can open its lid so you can see more clearly. Remember, you can ask the angels to open it for you. When your third eye is open, ask for the veil to be lifted between heaven and earth. Then breathe in as much light as you can from the divine spiritual sun into your third eye. Imagine the light coming through clearing all darkness. (Pause) Now, allow the wisdom and guidance of the divine to flow into your third eye so you can see clearly all that you need to know. Take a moment and think of a question you would like answered by divine guidance. (Pause) Then ask the angels to communicate the answer through your inner visions or by symbolic understanding. Be patient and know it will come. If you do not understand what they are trying to show you, ask for clarity. (Pause) Now thank the angels and ask them to help you keep your third eye open when it's appropriate.

Then slowly come back through your breath into the present moment, feeling clear, grateful, and at peace.

Clairaudience: "Clear Hearing"

It's not uncommon when you first start connecting with the angels and you hear the voice of divine guidance that your first thought is, "It's just my imagination and I am making it up." It is important to remember that the voice of the angels isn't necessarily an audio voice heard from outside of you. It can be a loving, supportive thought communicated through your mind. Sometimes it might feel like a whisper and other times it's loud and clear.

Here are some of the possible experiences of clairaudience:

☆ You hear someone calling your name but no one's there.
☆ You hear songs in your head and the words communicate a message to you.
☆ You are driving and you're lost and you hear a clear voice in your thoughts telling you where to go.
☆ You hear inspirational messages of love and guidance communicated through your thoughts.
☆ You hear a ringing or different tones playing in your inner ear.

Messages from your angels are always positive, uplifting, and encouraging. If you find the words you hear come from negativity or a place of fear, know that these are not messages from your angels. Most likely they come from your ego. If this happens, ask your ego to sit on the sidelines during meditation and spend some time raising your vibration so you can attune to the higher frequencies of divine guidance.

Exercise to Practice Clairaudience

Bring your journal or some paper and a pen to your quiet place. Set your intention that you are going to receive guidance from the angel about a specific question. Keep your writing materials on your lap and get comfortable. Close your eyes and take some nice deep breaths. Ask the angels to surround you in the protection and love of the divine white light. Breathe into this light and imagine that your mind, body, and spirit blend and become one with its magnificence. Then write on your piece of paper, "Dearest angels, please help me hear your words of wisdom and guidance to answer the following question." Then write your question and sit and listen to the words or messages that flow through your mind and thoughts. Even if you think you're making it up, write it down. Try not to think about it and just let your pen flow and allow it to record the thoughts and words that come to you. After your mind becomes quiet, stop and thank your angels. Read your message and notice how it feels.

Clairsentience: "Clear Feeling"

When you are clairsentient, your intuition speaks to you through your emotions and the physical sensations in your body. Many people who are empathetic (meaning if you are sensitive to the feelings of others around you) are naturally clairsentient. A typical comment from someone who is clairsentient is, "I just had a feeling" or, "I had a hunch."

Remember, the angels use your intuition to communicate their messages of guidance. So they can use your body and its sensations to get your attention. Set your intention that you are going to become more conscious of your feelings and the sensations in your body. Ask your angels to help you know the difference between a good feeling and a bad feeling. This information becomes very valuable. Your angels can then use your body as a messenger to guide you to your highest and best, better than you could ever imagine.

Here are some possible experiences of clairsentience:

☆ You feel a chill down your spine.
☆ You get a gut feeling about someone you just met.
☆ You have a strong feeling to call a friend and when you do, she needs to talk to you.
☆ You feel someone standing over your shoulder and no one is there.
☆ Without explanation, you are overcome with emotion.
☆ You experience a sudden change in room temperature.

Have you had any of these experiences and did you ever think it might be your angels trying to get your attention? Start turning inward to your senses and notice if your strongest clair is clairsentience. If you recognise this to be true, learn to trust your feelings and allow your intuition to guide you.

Angel Advice

If you are empathetic and sensitive to other people's feelings and emotions, it's important for you to learn to protect yourself. When you are stressed and your energy is low you are more vulnerable to other people's feelings and emotions. Ask your angels to replenish your energy and surround you with a shield of divine white light. This will increase your energy level and protect you from other people's negativity.

Fun Practice with Clairsentience

Look at the following scenarios and ask yourself, "Is this a good feeling leading to a positive experience or is this a negative feeling, which yields caution?"

1. You are contemplating taking a new job. You ask for guidance and you feel confusion and nausea.

2. You think or hear an inspirational idea and you feel a chill down your spine.

3. You're shopping for a new home and you enter a house which feels cold, uncomfortable, and you can't wait to leave.

4. You meet someone new at an event. You immediately feel comfortable and you talk for hours.

5. You go on a first date and you feel relaxed, comfortable, and you have butterflies in your stomach.

Your feelings are your inner compass. They can guide you in any situation so you can experience a positive outcome. Your job is to pay attention and learn to understand what your feelings are saying. If it's a not-so-good feeling, think again. If the feeling is peaceful or positive, go for it.

Claircognizance: "Clear Knowing"

Claircognizance is when you have an inner knowing about something or someone. When you use this sense of intuition you know what you are thinking or saying is true beyond any doubt. Many speakers, writers, artists, and inventors naturally use their gifts of claircognizance. They consciously or unconsciously tap into the divine mind for inspiration, creativity, and innovation. When you experience claircognizance, it feels as if your idea or inspiration comes from a higher source and you feel compelled to put it into action.

Here are some possible experiences of claircognizance:

★ You are talking to someone and you know exactly what she is going to say.
★ You receive an idea or inspiration about writing a book and you know you have to do it.
★ You know something about someone but you don't know how you know it.
★ You know beyond any doubt that you need to move to a particular place.
★ You knew all your life, since a young age, that you were going to be a teacher, mother, doctor, or another specific profession.

Have you had any of these experiences or would you like to? If so, pay attention to your ideas, inspirations, or your inner knowing. Learn to trust it and have the courage to act upon it. Know that everyone has the ability to become one with the divine mind. When you choose to, you access the unlimited resource of divine wisdom and knowledge.

Meditation and Prayer for Claircognizance

This is a meditation to open your crown chakra, the energy center at the top of your head. When it is open and clear, you can receive higher wisdom and knowledge from the angels. Before you start your meditation, share the following prayer with the angels:

Angel Prayer

"Dearest angels, please assist me in meditation to open and clear my crown chakra. My desire and intention is to open the channel of communication between myself and the divine so I may easily receive claircognizance information. I want to know beyond any doubt that this information is from a higher source of wisdom. Help me trust what I receive and give me the courage to act upon it for the highest and greatest good of all."

Now, in your sacred peaceful place for meditation, call upon the angels. Close your eyes and breathe one with their loving presence. Feel their desire to assist you. They have heard your prayer and they are working behind the scenes to help you in any way they can. As you breathe, imagine yourself lifting into the higher vibrations of light. Imagine yourself going right into the spiritual sun, where you connect to the oneness of the angels. (Pause) Take a few moments and give yourself permission to relax into this beautiful energy. (Pause) Now imagine the top of your head opening and allow the light in. Ask for the divine mind to fill your thoughts with the knowing and inspiration of the angels. There is nothing for you to do; just breathe in the light. Sit in quiet, relax and allow yourself to just receive. You are one with the divine mind. Trust that you will easily and effortlessly receive divine inspiration and knowing to assist you in all aspects of your life. (Pause and receive) Thank the angels for opening your crown chakra to receive divine wisdom. Share with them your desire to continue to receive clear knowing in your everyday life. Slowly, breathe back into the present moment with gratitude and clarity.

Clairgustance: "Clear Taste" and Clairolfactory: "Clear Smell"

These are two clairs that need to be mentioned, but the experiences of these psychic senses are not as common as the others. The reasoning for this can be that most people don't pay attention to smell and taste and so they might go unnoticed.

Clairolfactory is the ability to smell something even though it's not physically there. The most common experience of clairolfactory is when your deceased relatives are around you and you smell something familiar that reminds you of them. For example, the perfume your grandmother wore or the biscuits that your mother always baked

Clairgustance is the ability to taste something when there's nothing physically in your mouth to create that taste. Again, it's more common to experience this when your deceased loved ones are around you. Instead of smelling something you actually taste it. If all of a sudden you taste tobacco and you don't smoke and there is no one around you smoking, most likely you're sensing someone around you who smoked while he was alive but has now passed. Another experience of clairgustance is you suddenly taste salt water and you are nowhere near the ocean. Your angels might be trying to tell you it's time to go to the beach or take a holiday.

You can develop both of these senses just by paying attention and taking notice. If you taste or smell something that's not physically present, ask the angels to help you understand what it's connected to.

Enhancing Your Intuition and Psychic Abilities with the Angels

Spiritual Growth

*T*here is a difference between spirituality and religion. Religion offers a specific set of beliefs and rules for people to follow and be inspired by. Spirituality is more about your own personal relationship with the divine. You develop your own belief system based on what feels comfortable to you. Neither is right or wrong, good or bad.

It's important to follow the path that feels right for you. Honour your own personal belief system and be open to learning and growth. This is what spirituality is all about. The angels honor who you are and what you choose with unconditional love. They will work with you and help you enhance your abilities to communicate in your own personal way. Continue to communicate with them and tell them what you need.

Clear Communication Between You and the Divine

Because the angels want to communicate with you, they will assist you in clearing the different pathways so you can use your clairs to receive information. They can remove the fear and the confusion that hinders your ability to hear or see more clearly. They can help you raise your vibration so you can feel their messages of divine guidance and experience the clear knowing so you can take action accordingly.

The angels ask you to have the desire and intention to open up and receive their messages of divine guidance. This creates a powerful energy of co-creation, where together, you can create miracles.

Angel Prayer

A Prayer for Clear Communication

Dear angels, I have a profound desire to feel a deeper connection with you. Please help me clear the pathways of communication so I may easily receive your loving messages of divine guidance. My desire is to hear clearly, see clearly, and feel clearly. Help me understand and have a clear knowing of what the messages mean. Thank you for all your help as I journey toward a deeper connection with the divine.

Clearing and Removing the Blocks

The angels are here, right now, surrounding you in love and support. The veil of disbelief, fear, and negativity keeps you from feeling them, hearing them, seeing them, and knowing of their

truth. You can lift this veil by staying committed to your desire—
to know and experience the truth of the divine. Trust that the
angels will also work behind the scenes to clear the disbelief, fear,
and negativity. You can clear and remove the blocks in many ways.
Try the following:

☆ Use affirmations to transform your negative thoughts into
   positive manifestations. For example: Instead of saying, "I
   can't see anything when I meditate or ask for help," affirm, "I
   clearly see images, symbols, and visions and I understand what
   these messages mean."
☆ Meditate, pray, and ask the angels to clear your blocks so you
   can receive their messages.
☆ Ask the angels to heal your blocks during your dream state.
   Ask for their help before you go to sleep and then invite them
   to work on you while you sleep.
☆ Try alternative healing modalities: hypnosis, Reiki,
   breathwork, massage, or acupuncture.
☆ Clear your chakras, your energy centers that receive intuitive
   information.

   Any of these techniques will release the blocks. Experiment and
discover which ones work best for you. As you release and let go,
the channels of communication will open and your intuition will
heighten. It will be well worth the effort and the time you spend
healing what no longer serves you.

Chakra Clearing Meditation

The word chakra is Sanskrit for "wheel" or "disk." Your chakras are the energy centers in your body. There are seven of them and they are aligned from the crown of your head to the base of your spine. These energy centers are where you receive intuitive information from the divine. Clearing the chakras is a powerful way to open up the channels of communication.

Set your intention for the following meditation. Ask the angels to help you clear your chakras so you can enhance your intuition.

Find a quiet place to sit, and if you choose, select some peaceful meditation music to play in the background. Ask the archangels to surround you in a beautiful circle of light, love, and protection. (Pause) Sit upright and imagine a column of light connecting you to the heavenly light above to the core of the earth below. Imagine or see it running through your spinal column, grounding you from above to below. Just breathe with the divine white flowing through it. Imagine inhaling the energy up from the core of the earth and then exhaling it down from the heavens. Eventually it becomes one flowing breath. (Pause)

Now, focus on your first chakra at the base of your spine. This energy center is red, so imagine the color red spinning in your base chakra in a clockwise motion. Ask the archangels to clear any darkness in this chakra. (Pause) Then ask to bring any healing to this energy center so it flows with peace, light, and harmony. Affirm, "I am safe. All my needs are met. I am grounded to the physical plane. I am healthy and I am prosperous." (Pause)

Now, focus on your second chakra, located in the lower abdomen, and sexual organs. This energy center is orange, so imagine the colour orange spinning in your second chakra in a clockwise motion. Ask the archangels to clear any darkness in this chakra. (Pause) Then ask to bring any healing to this energy center so it flows with peace, light, and harmony.

Affirm, "I am able to accept change with ease. I am creative, passionate, and sensual." (Pause)

Now, focus on your third chakra, located in solar plexus. This energy center is yellow, so imagine the colour yellow spinning in your third chakra in a clockwise motion. Ask the archangels to clear any darkness in this chakra. (Pause) Then ask Archangel Raphael to bring any healing to this energy center so it flows with peace, light, and harmony.

Affirm, "I am comfortable being in my power. I am confident and I believe in myself." (Pause)

Now, focus on your fourth chakra, the heart chakra. This energy center is green, so imagine the color green spinning in your fourth chakra in a clockwise motion. Ask the archangels to clear any darkness in this chakra. (Pause) Then ask Archangel Raphael to bring any healing to this energy center so it flows with peace, light, and harmony.

Affirm, "I am loved and I love deeply. I am compassionate and I accept myself and others for who they are." (Pause)

Now, focus on your fifth chakra, the throat chakra. This energy center is blue, so imagine the colour blue spinning in your fifth chakra *in a clockwise motion. Ask the archangels to clear any darkness in this chakra. (Pause) Then ask to bring any this energy center so it flows with peace, light, and harmony. Affirm, "I can easily express myself and my feelings from a place of love. I am open to divine will." (Pause)*

Now, focus on your sixth chakra, the brow chakra or third eye chakra. This energy center is indigo, so imagine the colour indigo spinning in your sixth chakra in a clockwise motion. Ask the archangels to clear any darkness in this chakra. (Pause) Then ask the angels to bring any healing to this energy center so it flows with peace, light, and harmony. Affirm, "I easily see intuitive guidance from the divine. I am clear and open to see physically and intuitively." (Pause)

Now, focus on your seventh chakra, the crown chakra at the top of your head. This energy center is violet, so imagine the color violet spinning in your seventh chakra in a clockwise motion. Ask the archangel to clear any darkness in this chakra. (Pause) Then ask the angels to bring any healing to this energy center so it flows with peace, light, and harmony. Affirm, "I am one with the divine. I easily receive clear knowing and wisdom from the divine." (Pause)

When you are finished clearing your chakras, ask if there are any messages of divine guidance for you to receive at this time. (Pause) Then slowly breathe back into the present moment. Notice how clear and peaceful you feel. Say thank you to the archangels and be open to the divine guidance you receive throughout your day.

This is a wonderful meditation to do in the morning to start your day and before you do your angel readings. If you practice this meditation regularly you will enhance your intuition to new levels. Enjoy doing this practice and consider it as another tool for your spiritual toolbox.

Enhancing Your Psychic Abilities

Everyone has psychic abilities, even if they are unaware of these abilities. The *Merriam-Webster Dictionary* defines psychic as someone who is "sensitive to nonphysical or supernatural forces and influences." In other words, you are using your psychic abilities to connect with the angels.

Using your intuition and your psychic abilities are pretty much the same, except the term "psychic" has received a bad reputation over the years. When you use your psychic abilities you receive information about the past, present, and future. You can ask the angels for this information and they will communicate the answers to you by using your different clairs.

Here are some possible intuitive or psychic impressions you might receive from divine guidance:

⭑ The angels might show you a past memory from childhood as an answer to a prayer.

⭑ You might hear the angels giving you directions in the car to avoid an accident ahead. For example, "Slow Down" or "Move over to the right."

⭑ You might get a sick feeling in your stomach when you meet a new business associate.

* You might see your future home or future soul mate in detail during your meditation.
* You might have a dream about a past life that is giving you insight into a present situation.
* You might get a feeling that someone is going to pass into heaven very soon.

If you begin to receive these intuitive or psychic impressions and you feel nervous about getting this information, ask your angels to comfort you. They will reassure you that everything is okay. You would not be receiving this information if it wasn't meant to be. If you are unsure about the information, ask the angels to give you confirmation that this information is coming from a divine source. They will do everything in their power to make you feel comfortable and safe.

Receiving Future Insight

Have you ever wished you had a crystal ball to look into the future? Why do you think psychics are so popular? People want to know about their future because they are impatient and curious or maybe they just fear the unknown.

☆ ☆ ☆ ☆ ☆ ☆ ☆ ☆ ☆ ☆ ☆ ☆ ☆ ☆ ☆

Angel Advice

Take time and do your research before you go to just any psychic. Receiving information from someone who is not centered in the highest intention can be detrimental. If they share something "bad" (which divine guidance would not do), it can make a lasting impression and cause unnecessary stress and worry.

The angels will share information about your future when it's beneficial for you to know. They will also show you the path of the highest potential, but it's important to understand there are other paths to choose from. There is no right or wrong path; it's just a different experience based on the path you chose. Remember, you live in a world of free will and free choice. So if you are shown something about your future, you always have the power to choose differently.

If you would like insight into your future, ask the angels to provide you with this information. Then pay attention. Notice your dreams and significant signs or synchronicities. Ask for guidance during your meditation or use the angel cards to see if you can get any insight. If it's in your best interest to know, they will share this information with you. If not, trust in divine timing and stay conscious of the present moment.

Receiving Guidance in Your Dreams

Your dream time is a very sacred space for the soul to do its work. In essence, you are a spiritual being and you have the ability to return "home" and visit the angels during this time of rest. Anything is possible during your dream time: healing, learning, receiving insight into all aspects of your life, and connecting with the divine. You can utilise this valuable time and enhance your spiritual experiences during this altered state of consciousness. Divine helpers can assist you in the following ways:

★ Healing, both physical and emotional, can take place in your dreams.

★ Healing of your past in this lifetime and other lifetimes can take place in your dreams.

★ Insight that answers your prayers can take place in your dreams.

★ Seeing the future can take place in your dreams.

★ Meeting angels, guides, and loved ones can take place in your dreams.

★ Learning and spiritual growth can take place in your dreams.

Ask the angels to assist you in any and all of these ways. Before you go to sleep, invite them into your dream time and ask them to be your guides. Set your intention to remember your dreams and ask them to give you everything you need to know in order to interpret them. It is an honor for them to serve you. Work with them and discover how your eight hours of rest can become your magical time to visit heaven and receive some valuable insight.

Communicating with Loved Ones in Spirit

One of the most difficult things to go through is losing a loved one. The angels know this and they want to help. If you have lost a loved one, they will ease your pain so you can experience more peace and healing. One of the ways they can assist you in doing this is to help you communicate with your loved ones in heaven. It is only the veil between heaven and earth that separates you, and the angels can help you hear, feel, and see beyond the veil.

Trust that the angels can be your "mediums" in spirit. They can communicate for your loved ones or they can bring you to visit them in your dream state. Ask for their help in making that connection and ask that you receive validation that they are happy and at peace.

Angel Prayer

Prayer to Communicate with a Loved One

Angels, please help lift the veil so I can visit and connect to _____ (state your loved one's name). I am asking for undeniable validation that they are still with me. Let me know and feel that they are happy and peaceful in heaven. Please bring peace to all concerned. You know who _____ (state your loved one's name) is and you know how to bring us together. I trust that this will happen soon and I thank you in advance for this beautiful gift of peace and healing.

COMMUNICATING DIRECTLY WITH THE ANGELS

Creating a Sacred Space

Your sacred space is a place of retreat where you can step away from your busy everyday life. It's a quiet, peaceful place where you can connect with the loving presence and assistance of the angels. You don't need to wait until you have a whole room available. You can pick a favorite chair, a small corner of your home or apartment, a bench outdoors, or even the shower can be a perfect place to retreat where no one can bother you.

Angel Advice

A wonderful way to start your day is to enter your sacred space and ask the angels to fill your day with blessings. Ask them to show you what you need to know throughout the day. Enter again at night and release your worries and fears to the angels. Complete your day with gratitude and thank the angels for all that they do.

How do you create your sacred space? It's very personal and must be meaningful to you. Picture your sacred space as a little getaway where you can experience safety, peace, and clarity. Here are some suggestions for creating your sacred space:

* Play peaceful music.
* Display pictures of your favourite religious deities.
* Display pictures of your loved ones living or deceased.
* Light candles to create the energy.
* Place crystals or rocks collected from meaningful places.
* Place pictures or statues of angels.
* Find a special journal to write in.
* Have a fountain with the soothing sound of water.
* Turn the volume off on your phone.

After your sacred space is created, set your intention that this is your special place to come where you can let go, pray, and be open to the gifts and miracles of the angels. Each and every time you enter your space, invite the angels to gather and ask them to surround you in their loving light and protection. Ask them to fill your space with the highest vibration of divine white light and energy and know that with every breath that you take, you will become one with this sacred healing light.

Meditation

If you are curious to learn more and you are ready to open your heart to the angels, then make a point to schedule some quality time for meditation. You can start with ten minutes. Spend some time in prayer and share with the angels your concerns and requests. As you discover the benefits from taking this time for yourself, you might want to experiment with listening to a guided meditation CD or spend time writing your thoughts to the angels.

Another option is to seek out a meditation class or retreat. Some people benefit from the group energy atmosphere. It may help you to connect with other like-minded people and a facilitator who can give you some guidance and answer your questions. Trust and know that there is no right or wrong way to meditate; it's a matter of experimenting and discovering the best method for you.

Angel Advice

After you meditate or do intuitive exercises, ask the angels to "zip up" your energy field. You don't want to walk around wide open to receive psychic information from everyone. Ask the angels to protect you and request that they keep your clairs open only when it's in your best interest to receive this information.

Meeting Your Guardian Angel

Can you imagine what it would feel like to know that you are never alone and you have an angel watching over you and protecting you at all times? You have at least two guardian angels at the time of your birth and they will be with you until the time that you leave this earth plane. Remember, you have to ask your guardian angels to be a part of your life.

Ask the Angel

How can I know for sure that my guardian angel is there?
Ask for a sign from them to know beyond any doubt that they are there
to guide you along your journey. You can ask for a specific sign like a
rose or you can ask for something that is significant to you.

There are different ways to connect with your guardian angels. First, share your desires with them. If you want to meet them in your meditation or dream state, ask them to make their presence known to you. If you want to feel comforted by their love or you want to know that you are safe and protected, then ask your guardian angels to help you feel this. If you want to receive messages of guidance, ask them to help you hear their loving voices through your thoughts.

Meditation to Connect with Your Guardian Angel

Would you like to meet your guardian angel? Go to your sacred space and set the intention that you will meet your guardian angel.

Get comfortable and close your eyes and take a couple of deep breaths. (Pause) Let go of whatever happened before your meditation and do the same for whatever is going to take place after your meditation. This is your special time and you are going to meet your guardian angel. Now in your mind's eye, imagine yourself in a beautiful meadow: the sun's shining, it's a beautiful day, and nature is singing all around you. The beautiful soothing light from the sun relaxes you and comforts you. You can really let go and just be there. (Pause

As you look ahead, you see a beautiful path and you go toward the path, intrigued by where it may lead. As you follow the path you feel lighter and lighter. (Pause) It leads you into the most beautiful garden you have ever seen. This is your soul's garden. You can see, feel, and create all the beauty you desire in your garden. If you want waterfalls, there are waterfalls. If you desire animals, beautiful flowers and colours, it's all there. You create the garden of your wishes. Know that it's peaceful, it's sacred, and there is so much love in this garden. (Pause) Now, look for that perfect place to sit and rest. It could be a bench, a hammock, or you may just lie on the ground. (Pause) Know that as you sit in this beautiful place, your desire is to meet your guardian angel. Call out and ask your guardian angel to come close so you can feel or see her presence and know beyond any doubt that this is your guardian angel. Sit in silence, breathe, and receive. (Pause)

When you're ready, ask your guardian angel if she has a message for you. (Pause) Ask that your guardian angel continue to guide you to the answers to your prayers. Share if there is anything you need help with. Thank your guardian angel and express your desire that you would like your guardian angel to continue to make her presence known to you.

Writing with Your Angels

Journaling with your angels can be both healing and enlightening. Some people do very well with this technique of communication. Writing the messages might make it easier for you to bypass your intellectual mind so you can allow the pen to record the angelic thoughts flowing through your consciousness.

One way to start is to clear your mind. You can do this by writing on paper all the thoughts that go through your mind. They can be mundane like, "I loved my cup of coffee this morning" or they can be filled with stress and fear like, "I don't know how I am going to pay my mortgage this month." Just write and fill the pages until the pen stops or your mind quiets.

After your mind is clear, turn to a blank page and write at the top of the page, "My dearest angels, what would you like to say to me today?" Then breathe in the love of the angels all around you, listen, feel, and write down whatever comes to you. If you get images or colours, write them down. If you just get words, write them down. If you receive feelings, record the feeling.

Trust that as you put your pen to the paper and you start writing, the words will come. Try not to think about what you are writing and certainly don't concern yourself with spelling, just write and let it flow.

Asking a Specific Question

You can also use writing to ask your angels to answer a specific question. Again, clear your mind through meditation or release your thoughts by writing them on paper. Then ask your angels to guide you during your writing session and ask them to lead you to your highest and best. On a blank piece of paper, write at the top, "Dearest angels, please give me your guidance on the following question (then write your question)." Breathe with the angels, listen, feel, and write down anything that comes to you. When you read your message, notice how it feels. If it is loving, encouraging, and supportive then this is a message from your angels. Then ask for guidance, ask for peace and allow yourself to receive the answers you are searching for. Trust that these messages can flow easily through the clarity of your thoughts onto the paper.

Angel Mail

This is a very powerful yet playful way to communicate with your angels. The angels want you to surrender your worries and prayers to them so they can help you.

When you hold on so tight to your issues or when you want to control the outcome of your life, you get in your own way and it's harder for the angels to help you. Sending angel mail is a wonderful way to let go and ask for help. Write a letter to your angels and share your prayers, worries, and concerns, both for yourself and others. Then put it in an envelope and symbolically or literally address it to the angels. As you send it, surrender it and trust that it will be read and heard. Ask for divine resolution to occur and then let it go.

Ask the Angel

I am only getting words and not sentences.
Am I doing something wrong?

No, there is no right or wrong way to communicate with the angels.
Words can be very powerful. Listen and pay attention to the words you
received. If you practice, words will eventually flow into sentences.

This is also a wonderful technique for children to use. They can
colour or write their prayers or fears on paper and together you
can send it to the angels. Imagine if you can teach a child from
a very young age that they can let go of what's bothering them.
Remind that they can go to the angels for help. After you
share this gift with your child, watch the peace on their face as
they put the letter in the postbox.

Talking to Your Angels in the Car

Life can be crazy, running from one thing to the other. If you can
relate to this and your day is filled with responsibilities and an
endless to-do list, then this method of connecting with the angels
is perfect for you.

The angels are everywhere and they are even present while you
are driving in your car. So make the car your sacred space. Turn off
the radio and invite your angels into your car. Ask your guardian

angel to sit in the passenger seat and ask your other angels to fill the back seat. Then breathe with the comfort and support of knowing they are there with you. The angels are great listeners, so share with them your worries, fears, and concerns. Ask for the help you need so you can experience peace, balance, and joy.

It sounds so simple, but this time can be precious for those on the go. You will find that spending this time in silence and communion with your angels will create blessings throughout your entire day.

Dream with the Angels

The average person spends eight hours a day sleeping, so this time can be used very wisely when working with the angels. During your time of sleep your conscious mind steps back, and because of this, you can get out of your own way so you can open up to other realms of consciousness. Before you go to sleep at night, ask the angels to enter your dream state. Ask them to help you remember what you dreamed the night before.

Angel Advice

If you tend to have scary dreams or you are afraid of opening up in your dreamtime, before you go to sleep ask the angels to keep you safe and protected. If you are experiencing precognitive dreams (dreaming about future events), ask the angels to help you remember only what you need to know.

You can ask for help with the following in your dream state:

* Ask the angels for any healing you need, physical, emotional, or mental.
* Ask the angels to help you connect with your loved ones in spirit so you can receive a message that they are okay.
* Ask the angels for guidance about anything in your life.
* Ask the angels for spiritual teaching or help in learning what you need to know to further your development.
* Ask the angels to help you travel to other places and other times.
* Ask the angels to help you connect with them and any other guides or divine helpers that want to work with you.

Affirm before you go to bed, "Dearest angels, please enter my dreamtime tonight and help me with healing and share with me your clear messages of divine guidance (ask a specific question if you like). Please help me remember whatever I need to know when I awaken. Thank you." Keep a dream journal by your bed and when you wake up, record all your thoughts and impressions from the night before. You may be able to interpret some dreams immediately, while other dreams may be more symbolic and you might not understand them in that moment. Continue to record your dreams and in time your symbolism will transform into meaningful insight.

How to do Angel Card Readings

Why Use Angel Cards?

Angel cards are tools. You can have some fun with the cards and, at the same time, you can enhance your relationship with the angels as you learn more about them. Use the cards as educational tools to help you learn more about the different roles the angels play and how they can help you in your life. For those of you who have a hard time hearing messages of divine guidance on your own, the cards can provide the clarity you need.

Most of the cards on the marketplace have helpful words and images. Each deck usually comes with a book that gives a description and detailed information about each card along with a message of divine guidance. Angel cards are very different from tarot cards. They can act as a guide just like tarot cards, but angel cards have no negativity and there is nothing to fear. Angel cards reflect the positive, loving, and encouraging messages of the angels. They are a wonderful tool and they can help you gain clarity about anything and everything in your life.

Choosing Your Angel Cards

Take time to shop for your angel cards. It's very important to feel connected with your deck just as you want to feel connected with your angels. Most stores will have open boxes so you can actually look at the decks. Pay attention to the images, the messages, and the feelings you get when you look at the cards. Trust that you will know and find the perfect deck for you.

You can also find some sites online where you have the option to choose an individual angel card or a series of angel cards by simply clicking on the featured deck. This is a great tool to get an idea of which decks resonate with you before you go out and purchase one.

Finding the perfect deck of cards for you is an adventure. Be curious and explore your options. Once you've found your perfect deck you will be pleasantly surprised. You will have a valuable tool in your spiritual toolbox that enhances your ability to connect with the angelic realm so you can receive loving messages of divine guidance.

Getting to Know Your Deck

Once you've selected your deck, take some time to get familiar with the cards. They each have their own significance and meaning. The more you know and understand about the meaning of the cards, the easier they are to work with.

There are several ways you can get to know your deck. Here are some suggestions you can try:

★ Read the entire booklet that comes with your deck describing each card and its significant meaning.

★ Pick one card at a time and learn the meaning of that card.

★ Pick a card and before you read the booklet, write to the angels and ask them for the message and meaning of each card. (After you've finished writing, you can always go back and see what the book says.)

★ Pick a card and place it by your bedside or under your pillow. Ask the angels to teach you the meaning of the card during your dream state.

The more you play with your cards and discover the meaning of their messages, the clearer the lines of communication become. The angels can use the cards to get your attention and to provide you with the answers to your prayers. The results will be well worth the time you spent getting to know your deck.

Gaining Insight from the Cards

The angel cards can become a helpful tool to communicate with the angels. You can use the cards to receive insight and to ask questions about all aspects of your life: relationships, finances, health, emotional well-being, life purpose, career, and other everyday questions. When you pick your cards you may understand immediately what the cards are trying to tell you. At other times you may need to pause for reflection to gain a full perspective on the messages. The following are some of the possible insights that you may receive from your reading:

★ The reading may reveal an immediate answer to a prayer.

★ The reading may suggest that you need to make some changes in your life.

★ The reading might initiate healing: physical, emotional, mental, or spiritual.

★ The reading might open your awareness so you can pay attention to the angels.

★ The reading might provide you with the help and guidance you are seeking.

★ The reading may give you direction or reveal steps to take that will lead you to the answer to your prayers.

★ The reading may provide you with a feeling of peace, that you are right where you are meant to be and all is well.

Everyone has questions they would like answered. That's why psychics are so popular and so many people go to see them. But what if you could go to the angels and receive their loving guidance through the use of the cards? You could ask your questions and you would feel a sense of peace that the cards were guiding you with supportive insight. Experiment with the cards and see for yourself how it feels. Seek to discover if this is a good tool for you to communicate with the angels.

Preparing for an Angel Reading

Any time you pick cards or do an angel reading you want to create your sacred space and set your intention. Invite the angels into your sacred space and ask them to help you through the use of the cards. They are happy to assist you in any way they can. You can use the following steps to prepare for your angel reading:

1. Bring your journal or some paper to your sacred space.
2. Play some peaceful or angelic music in the background.
3. Close your eyes and always surround yourself with divine

white light and protection.

4. Invoke your angels and ask them to surround you in a beautiful circle of love, light, and healing. Take a few moments and breathe as one with the angels and their loving presence.

5. Do a meditation that will raise your vibration so you can attune to their energy. (It does not have to be a long meditation; it's all about intention.)

6. When you are ready to do your reading, ask the angels to help you through the use of the cards. Ask them to guide you to the answers you are looking for.

Picking Angel Cards

Picking an angel card is a fun and insightful way to connect with your angels and to receive a message of divine guidance. You can pick an angel card to answer a specific question or you can just ask for guidance on what you need to know in that moment.

For example, "Dearest angels, what do I need to know today?" or you can ask a specific question. For example, "What do I need to know about_____?"

Take the follow steps to do a one-card reading:

1. Remember, always ask your angels to surround you in divine white light and energy before you pick a card.

2. Hold your deck of cards in your hands and say a prayer to receive a message that will guide you to your highest and best, better than you could ever imagine. (If you are asking a specific question, then state the question and ask that you be guided to the best card that will answer your question.)

3. Spread your cards out on the table. Then breathe and ask your angels to help you pick the perfect card. You can always look at the cards and see which card jumps out at you or you can pass your hand slowly across the cards. Feel through the energy in your hands and notice where your hand is drawn to and then pick that card.

4. After you select your card, you might have a clear meaning of what the card is telling you. If not, read the book that comes with the deck or ask the angels to help you understand what it means.

5. Thank your angels and ask that they continue to guide you.

It may seem as if the card you selected doesn't have any significant meaning. If this happens, write down the card that you picked in your journal and stay in tune to the angels. Pay attention during the upcoming week. Most likely the card's meaning will be revealed in the next couple of days or by the end of the week.

Reading for Past, Present, and Future

Now that you've learned how to pick an angel card and receive a message of divine guidance, you are ready to move on to experience a three-card angel reading. The intention of this reading is to receive insight and guidance about your past, present, and future. Most people want to know what their future holds, but it's important to realise how your past may still influence your present and the future. The greatest gift you can give yourself from this reading is to learn from the cards and allow them to give you the direction you need to live your best life in the present moment.

Take these steps to do a reading to receive insight about your past, present, and future:

1. Ask your angels to surround you in divine white light and energy before picking your cards.

2. Hold your deck of cards in your hands and say a prayer asking to receive insight and guidance about your past, present, and future so you can be guided to your highest and best, better than you could ever imagine.

3. Spread your cards out on the table. Then breathe and ask your angels to help you pick the perfect cards. The first card is about the past. Choose your card and place it face-side up. The second card is about something significant or something you need to know about your present life. Choose your card and place it to the right (it will be your middle card). The last card is about your future and this card gets placed to the right of your present card. All cards can be faced right-side up.

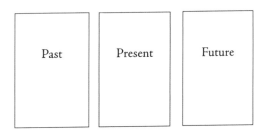

4. Take a few minutes and look at your spread of cards and ask the angels for guidance. Listen, feel, and ask for the clarity you

need. If it is helpful, use the book enclosed with your deck of cards for further insight.

5. Close the reading by thanking your angels and asking them to continue to guide you so you may fully understand the significance of your reading.

6. If some of your cards don't make sense at the time of your reading, record your cards and review them at a later time. Trust that you will receive exactly what you need from your reading.

Each card shares a message or a story about what you need to know. The past card is very important. It shares information from your past that could help you heal or better your life in the present and the future. Your present card asks you to pay attention to what's happening in your life right now. Your future card is sending you a message about an opportunity or a healing that might take place down the road.

Angel Advice

It is always important to use discernment when doing a card reading. If the cards you pick don't feel right or you really don't understand the meaning of the cards, then reshuffle them and pray with the angels and ask for help in picking new cards.

☆ ☆ ☆ ☆ ☆ ☆ ☆ ☆ ☆ ☆ ☆ ☆ ☆ ☆ ☆

Use this reading when you want to receive clarity or you need help understanding a current life situation. It will provide you with the insight you need to make better decisions, to take appropriate action or to just pay attention. Most often, you will finish your reading with a sense of peace and understanding.

Reading for Different Aspects of Your Life

Most people who come for an angel reading are looking for answers about certain areas of their lives. The most common questions asked are about relationships, career or life purpose, health and well-being, and finances. The following angel card reading will help you answer these questions, and it will also give you the opportunity to ask a specific question to be answered by divine guidance. Take the following steps to gain insight on these different aspects of your life:

1. Take the steps you've learned for preparing for an angel reading. Always ask your angels to surround you in divine white light and energy before picking your cards.

2. Hold your deck of cards in your hands and say a prayer asking to receive insight and guidance about your life so you can be guided to your highest and best, better than you could ever imagine.

3. Spread your cards out on the table. Breathe and ask your angels to help you choose the perfect cards as you pick with the following intentions.

4 The first card you choose is about relationships. You can ask about a specific relationship or you can ask for guidance about

your relationships in general. Choose your card and face it right-side up.

5. The second card is about career or life purpose. Choose your card and place it to the right of the first card you picked.

6. The third card is about health or emotional well-being and this card gets placed to the right of your career and life purpose card.

7. The fourth card you choose is about a question of your choice and this card is placed at the end of the other cards. All cards can be faced right-side up.

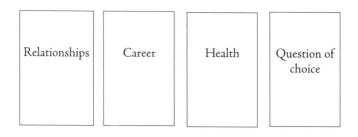

| Relationships | Career | Health | Question of choice |

8. Take a few minutes and look at your spread of cards and ask the angels for guidance. Listen, feel, and ask for the clarity you need. If it is helpful, use the book enclosed with your deck of cards for further insight.

9. Close the reading by thanking your angels and asking them to continue to guide you so you may fully understand the significance of your reading.

After you finish your reading take some time for reflection. See if the guidance you received can empower you to make some decisions or choices that will help you create the life you desire. God and the angels want you to live a life filled with peace, joy, happiness, health, and fulfillment. Allow this reading to be your compass guiding you in this direction.

Can You Do a Reading for Someone Else?

You can absolutely do an angel reading for someone else. It's recommended that you do readings for yourself first and really get to know your cards. Practice is the key. Each time you do a reading for yourself you expand your knowledge about the angels and their messages. With experience you gain confidence. This is exactly what you need to best facilitate an angel reading for another. Take the following steps when facilitating a reading for another person:

1. Explain what an angel reading is and how it can help them. Be sure to mention that the messages from the angels are always filled with positive thoughts, unconditional love, and encouragement.

2. Ask for permission to hold their hands. Your hands are faced palms up, because you are facilitating the reading. Ask both of your angels to create a beautiful circle of love, light, healing, and protection around you. Then breathe one with the angels' loving presence and relax and trust that they will guide you.

3. Ask the person you are reading for to take a deep breath and as they exhale, ask them to let go of everything that happened before the reading (you do the same). Then ask them to take another breath and as they exhale, ask them to let go of everything that's

going to happen after their reading. Then together breathe in the present moment.

4. Set the following intention either silently or with your partner: "Dearest angels, guide me so I can give a reading for (say the person's name). Allow me to receive the guidance I need for her highest and best, better than they could ever imagine."

5. Release your hands. Then decide or ask them if they want a one-card reading: a reading about past, present, and future; or a reading for the different aspects of their life.

6. Have them shuffle the deck or you can shuffle it for them. Spread out the cards and guide them to choose the number of cards needed to do the reading.

7. Take a few minutes and look at the cards. Ask the angels for help so you can share in their wisdom and guidance for the person you are doing a reading for. Listen, feel, and ask for the clarity you need. If it is helpful, use the book enclosed with your deck of cards for further insight.

8. After you complete the reading ask the other person if they understand the messages shared. If they seem confused about certain cards or messages shared, ask them to be open to their angels' guidance. Explain that they might not understand the meaning of the message now, but it is very possible that the clarity will come in the next couple of days or near future.

9. Give thanks to the angels and ask them to continue to help and guide the person you did a reading for. Share and encourage them to be open to the miracles ahead of them and to pay attention to how the angels might be trying to get their attention. It is important to remember that after you facilitate the reading you

need to disconnect from the energy of the other person. Your intention was to help them during the angel reading and now you need to release them to the angels. Imagine yourself "unplugging" from their energy just like unplugging a lamp from electricity. Trust it's in the highest and best of both of you to release and let go.

Angel Advice

Another way to receive guidance from the cards is to look at the illustrations expressed on the card. It can provide you with some valuable insight that you might not find in the words written on the cards or in the book enclosed with the deck.

It can be very rewarding when you share the angels' messages of love with another. Many people say that their life has been touched in a positive way after an angel reading. You will witness the other person experiencing a sense of peace and a knowing that they are never alone. The reading will reassure them that the angels are watching over them and are there to help in any way they can.

SYNCHRONICITY, SIGNS AND COINCIDENCES FROM THE ANGELS

Angels' Nudges

*H*ave you been asking the angels to help you? If so, it's time to start learning how they might be trying to get your attention so they can guide you to the answers you are seeking. The angels are always working behind the scenes in your favour. Sometimes it's through gentle nudges. For example, you're stuck and you need a babysitter for the kids. You pray to the angels for help and minutes later your friend calls and offers to take your kids. Think about it: Maybe the angels planted your name in her thoughts so she would call you.

Angel Prayer

An affirmation that will help you notice the angels' nudges:
"Dearest angels, please get my attention and show me what I need to know. Help me see, hear, and experience the miracles of your love and guidance throughout my day. Thank you."

Other times the nudge might bonk you over the head. For example, you know the next step in your career is to get certified in a certain specialty and you ask your angels for help because you need the finances to pay for the course. Within the next week, you receive an unexpected cheque in the mail that covers the expense of the entire course.

Angels help sometimes in small ways and other times it seems like a miracle. Be open to all their loving nudges and get ready to experience the magic of heaven on earth unfolding before your very eyes.

What Is Synchronicity?

Synchronicity is a coincidental occurrence of two or more events that have no relevance to one another, yet when it takes place it has great meaning to the person who is witnessing or experiencing it. The person who experiences a synchronistic event has previously said a prayer or they had a thought or a dream that later comes to fruition. They witness something that confirms what once was only an image or thought in their psyche. When this happens to you, you need to pay attention. This may be a form of divine communication where the angels are trying to give you a message or they want your attention.

What Is a Coincidence?

The word "coincidence" is actually two words, "co" and "incidence," which means when two things happen at the same time for no apparent reason. The meaning of coincidence is very similar to that of synchronicity, except when you experience a synchronicity, it is coincidence with meaning or significance. Here are some ways the angels work through coincidences:

★ The angels are trying to get your attention. Example: You keep finding dropped coins all around the house in the most obscure places.

★ The angels are reassuring you that you are not alone. Example: You have asked the angels to make their presence known to you and you see angel pictures and statues wherever you go.

★ The angels are trying to point you in the direction that will lead you to your highest and best. Example: You have asked the angels if it's in your best interest to go back to school and get your degree and that same week you receive a brochure in the post from the college you were considering.

★ The angels are answering a prayer. Example: You ask the angels to send you the perfect solicitor to help you through your divorce; you meet someone at an event and she shares that her husband is a divorce solicitor.

Experiencing coincidences can be magical and they can also validate that there is someone guiding you from the other side. Start noticing them and allow the angels to guide you through their gentle nudges so you can experience more peace, fulfillment, joy, and prosperity. It's all there waiting for you. Imagine that coincidences are gifts from the angels so you can manifest your dreams into reality.

What Is a Sign?

A sign is a confirmation from your angels. You can ask for a sign when you want the angels to validate their presence in your life. A good example of asking for a sign is that you did the meditation in this book to meet your guardian angel, but after you finished, you weren't quite sure if it was real. Then you ask your guardian angel to give you a sign that would confirm her presence. Watch for and pay attention to some of the following signs:

✴ Dropped pennies from heaven.
✴ White feathers.
✴ Angel trinkets or religious medals found in spontaneous places.
✴ Strange animals appearing out of nowhere.
✴ Smelling roses or flowers when none are present.
✴ Hearing a song on the radio about angels or one that has significant meaning.
✴ A street sign or a billboard with a message.
✴ The phone ringing but no one is there.
✴ Blinking lights or electrical items turning on and off.
✴ Angel lights or forms appearing in your pictures.

It's an amazing experience to witness any of these signs. They are all around you if you only notice and the more you notice, the more signs you experience.

Asking for a Sign

How do you ask for a sign? First, you need to decide if you want a specific sign from the angels, such as a rose or a butterfly, or if you want to leave it to the angels to decide. Either way, tell the angels you want your sign to be recognisable beyond any doubt. It's important that you know for sure that the sign you receive is from your angels.

Second, tell your angels that you want your sign delivered by a certain day or time. This is especially important for those of you who are impatient or if you need to make a decision within a certain period of time.

Lastly, surrender your request to your angels and pay attention. Keep your eyes, ears, and heart open so you can expand your awareness to receive your sign. When you have received your sign, thank the angels.

Another time you can ask the angels for a sign is when you need a specific question answered or you need confirmation to make a decision about something. Share your situation with the angels and tell them you want your question answered or confirmed with a specific sign.

Ask the Angel

What if I didn't get a sign from my angels?

The angels might want you to look again at the decision or question you asked about. There might be a better direction they want you to contemplate or explore. If you have any more questions, go into meditation and ask the angels for clarity.

Angel Numbers

The angels can also use numbers and the sequence of numbers to get your attention. Most people have a favourite number and the angels know your number. If they are trying to get your attention, you might notice your favourite number on a license plate or it could be the address of the house you pass.

There are two well-known, specific angelic numbers to pay attention to, and when you see them, it could be a sign from your angels. The numbers are 1111 and 444. So when you see these numbers on a clock, in a phone number, or even on a cheque, feel reassured that the angels are all around you.

Angel messages for number sequences from *Angel Numbers* by Doreen Virtue, PhD and Lynnette Brown:

✶ 111: An energetic gateway has opened for you rapidly manifesting your thoughts into reality. Choose your thoughts wisely at this time, ensuring that they match your desires. Don't put any energy into thinking about fears at all, lest you manifest them."

* 222: Have faith, everything's going to be all right. Don't worry about anything as this situation is resolving itself beautifully for everyone involved.

* 333: You're with the ascended masters, and they're working with you day and night—on many levels. They love, guide, and protect you in all ways.

* 444: Thousands of angels surround you at this moment, loving and supporting you. You have nothing to fear—all is well.

* 555: Major changes and significant transformations are here for you. You have an opportunity to break out of the chrysalis and uncover the amazing life you truly desire.

* 666: It's time to focus on Spirit to balance and heal your life. Tell heaven about any fears you have concerning material supply. Be open to receiving help and love from both humans and the angels.

* 777: Congratulations! You've listened well to your divine guidance and have put that wisdom into fruitful action. You're now reaping the rewards. Your success is inspiring and helping others, so please keep up the good work.

* 888: The universe is abundant and generous, and you have learned how to step into the shower of its ever-present flow. Great financial success is yours, now and in the future.

* 999: Get to work, Lightworker! The world needs your divine life purpose right now. Fully embark upon your sacred mission without delay or hesitation.

From this moment forward be conscious of the numbers that grab your attention. They could be a sign from your angels trying to get your attention or maybe they just want to send their love and reassure you that you are not alone.

Pay Attention

Once you ask the angels to guide you through signs, synchronicities, and coincidences, you need to play your part, and that is, to open your awareness and pay attention. The answers are already there for you to discover.

Angel Prayer

Affirmation to expand your awareness: "Dearest angels, please help me to be open so I can clearly recognize and notice the gifts of divine guidance all around me."

The angels have always been there. Now, you are choosing to see and experience them. You are opening up to different ways in which they can help you. You are expanding your awareness and you're noticing how they try to get your attention so they can communicate with you. All of a sudden you begin to witness the angels working their miracles all around you.

Notice Repetition

When you are not paying attention and the angels are trying to get their message across, they might use a little humor to help you take notice; it's called repetition. Have you ever heard the saying, "Pay attention when things happen in threes"? For example, within a matter of days three different people mention the same person. Maybe this is a sign to get in touch with that person.

The angels don't give up on you. So if you hear the same thing repeated over and over again in your head, listen to it and act upon it. When you experience repeated coincidences, synchronicities, or dreams around the same theme, pay attention because the angels are trying to tell you that it's important. Once you have noticed the repetition and you've acted accordingly or healed the situation, it will stop.

Angel Advice

If you are experiencing repetitive dreams, ask the angels to help you understand what the dream is trying to tell you. Some dreams are there to help you heal. So if there is healing that needs to take place, ask the angels to help you heal the root cause of the dream.

You can also ask the angels to reassure you with repetition when you don't trust the answers you are getting. For example, you have a major decision to make and you received a sign that affirmed your answer but you are still afraid of moving forward. Ask the angels to give you more confirmation so you can be reassured about making your decision.

Record the Magical Moments

When you walk your spiritual path and you open up to the angels, the world around you transforms into a magical place. Just imagine entering a fairytale where heaven and earth coexist.

No matter where you are along your journey, there is so much more for you to experience. The magic will continue to unfold and multiply if you choose. If you would like to initiate this energy, start a Magical Moments journal and record all the signs, coincidences, synchronicities, and miracles that occur around you. This practice will not only expand your awareness, but will also multiply your experience of the magic.

As you record your magical moments in your journal, you begin to see how the angels are guiding you to the answer to your prayers. You gain clarity and confidence and you allow these magical moments to be signposts from heaven guiding you to your highest and best, better than you could ever imagine.

Everyday Help from the Angels

Everyday Life Stuff

*L*ife is a journey and every day is a new experience. Sometimes life is predictable, and you understand your responsibilities and what to expect from your day. Then there are other days, where life can be unpredictable. You experience minor challenges that cause you stress and throw you off balance. For example, your alarm clock doesn't go off, you get stuck in traffic, your boss is in a bad mood, or the kids are fighting. Other challenges may have a greater affect on your life. For example, a death or sickness in the family, a change or loss of job, a divorce, or a local or world event that may directly distress you and your family. Whatever the experience may be, the angels know you have good days and bad days and they are willing to help you in any way they can.

Here are some different ways you can ask the angels to help you throughout your day:

✶ Before you get out of bed in the morning, ask the angels to help you create a day filled with ease and grace.

✶ If you're running late, ask the angels to stretch time or ask them to intervene so you can get where you need to go and still be on time.

✶ If you are worried about anything that's going to take place during your day, surrender it to the angels and ask for their help.

✶ Ask the angels to surround you with divine white light so no negativity from others can affect you.

★ On your way home from work, release your day to the angels and give all your cares and worries to them so you can go home and relax.

★ If you're worried about someone during your day, pray to the angels and ask them to watch over that person.

★ If you want to enjoy a peaceful night's sleep, surrender your day to the angels and ask for any help you need for anything left unresolved.

Make a point throughout your day to check in and notice how you feel. If things are flowing and you feel calm, be grateful. If you need help from the angels, stop and consciously ask for what you need. Over time you will realise you have the power to shift your experience in any given moment, no matter what's happening around you.

Gaining Patience

One of the meanings of patience is, "to suffer with strength of mind and courage." Another meaning is, "to hold steadfast in the midst of difficulty." Maybe that's why they say patience is a virtue; because it takes strength to hold back and breathe when you feel things are out of your control or you can't see the outcome of what's going to happen.

One of the most common messages of divine guidance is that of patience. The angels ask you to trust in divine timing and that everything is happening for a reason. Most people want to be in control, and when they feel things are out of their control they suffer. When this happens the angels will step in and remind you to have patience. This patience could be about your own personal growth and goals or about other people with whom you need to practice patience. You may be asked to accept them for who they are and not to judge their choices. It's important to remember that when you practice patience, you experience compassion and peace both for yourself and others.

Angel Advice

If you are experiencing repetitive dreams, ask the angels to help you understand what the dream is trying to tell you. Some dreams are there to help you heal. So if there is healing that needs to take place, ask the angels to help you heal the root cause of the dream.

Exercise to Practice Patience

Think of something going on in your life right now that requires patience. Take out your journal or a piece of paper. Ask your angels to surround you and breathe one with their love. Then write the following question: "Dearest angels, is there anything I can do today that will bring me more peace?" Listen, feel, and allow the answer to come. When you finish, ask the angels if there are any action steps you can take. If the angels share with you that you need to be patient and they advise you to accept what is right now, pray for patience and surrender the issue to the angels for divine resolution. Know that you have the power to choose peace in any moment. Simply affirm, "I am patient, and the angels will show me what I need to know."

Releasing Worry

How much time do you spend worrying about things that are out of your control? Do you ever look back and realise how much time and energy you spend on wasted worry? If you think about it, most of the time, you end up worrying about something that never happens. If you take worry to an extreme, it can mentally exhaust you and cause you physical illness.

Some worries are justified and can help you make better choices. For example, the doctor says you're overweight and because you worry you choose to eat better and exercise. There are the worries that cause needless stress such as worrying about what other people think or obsessing during the day about whether you locked the door when you left the house or worrying about the safety of your teenager who is driving in the snow. When it comes to worry, the angels can help you. Your job is to recognise it and then choose to release it to the angels.

Follow these steps to release your worry and ask for help from the angels:

1. Recognise and acknowledge your worry. Spend a couple of days being conscious and record all the things you worry about—both your minor and major worries.

2. Sit with your list and ask yourself, "How does it make me feel to worry about these things?"

3. Next, take a look at your list again and ask yourself, "How many of those things I feared or worried about actually happened?"

4. Take responsibility. Is there anything on your list that you are worried about that's within your control and you can affect? If so, list your action steps.

5. Surrender the rest of your worries to the angels. Let go and let them find the divine resolution.

You can use this powerful visualisation to release worry. Imagine the angels want to help you by giving you a worry basket. They ask you to release all your worries into the basket, both big and small. Next, imagine they lift your worries and they carry the basket into the divine light.

Every time you let go of worry you free your mind, body, and spirit. Not only do you free yourself but you also help all those people you once worried about. Think about it: If you send fear and worry to others, what do you imagine they feel? Reflect on how they might feel after you ask the angels for help and you release them from your fear and worry. Trust that the angels will watch over them and they will feel loved and protected. What a gift you give them by choosing to surrender your worry.

Negative Thoughts to Positive

Your thoughts create your experiences and your reality. When your thoughts are positive you create happiness, joy, fulfillment, and peace. If your thoughts are focused on the negative you can create fear, sickness, and stress. This is why it's so important to stay conscious of your thoughts and when you are focused on the negative, call out to the angels for help.

Angel Advice

When you catch yourself focusing on the negative or thinking about something you don't want to experience, say, "Cancel, cancel." This affirms that you are stopping the energy of your thoughts from going out into the universe to take on form or to reach other people.

The angels will encourage you to raise your vibration from negative thinking to positive thinking. Here are some ways to shift your energy and thoughts to the positive:

- When you're focused on lack or what you don't have, focus on the blessings in your life.
- Change your negative thoughts into positive affirmations. Say or write them daily until you create what you do want.
- When you're feeling doubtful or afraid, spend time in meditation with the angels. Spend time visualising and feeling

what you do want to experience.
* If you have negative thoughts about another person, send love
  to them and pray for them.
* Be conscious of your negative self-talk and when you catch
  yourself, say something kind and loving to yourself.
* Keep a gratitude journal and express gratitude every day.

As Norman Vincent Peale said, "Change your thoughts and you change your world." You have the power to do this and the angels will help you in any way they can. Make a commitment to yourself that you will pay attention to your thoughts. Focus on kind and loving thoughts toward yourself, others, and the world.

Gaining Peace with the Angels

Peace is a feeling, and you experience it when you're calm in mind, body, and spirit. Choosing your thoughts carefully is a step toward peace, but making choices and taking action to create more peace in your life is equally important.

Once you realise there's a situation in your life that's causing you pain, sadness, or stress, it's time to step back and reflect. Ask this question: "What do I really want and what will bring me peace?" Sometimes peace requires change, and change can be scary. Call on the angels for courage and ask them to support and guide you as you make the necessary changes in order to move forward.

Peace is a choice, and in any moment you can choose to experience peace. It doesn't matter where you are, who you are with, or what's going on, you can always choose to stop and

☆ ☆ ☆ ☆ ☆ ☆ ☆ ☆ ☆ ☆ ☆ ☆ ☆ ☆ ☆

breathe. As you take that precious breath, ask the angels to surround you in peace and then affirm, "I choose peace. I am peaceful."

Angel Prayer

Prayer for Peace

Dearest angels, I call on you now to help me find peace in this situation (share your situation with the angels). I realize peace is found in the moment, so please help me stay present in this moment, knowing that I am okay right here and right now (breathe with the angels). Help me become one with peace in my mind, body, and spirit. I surrender this situation to divine intervention and I trust that all is well.

Thank you, angels, for this gift of peace and for your continued love and support.

Lighten Up with the Angels

Are you feeling overworked, underpaid, or unfulfilled? Are you taking life too seriously and feeling overwhelmed with responsibilities? If this is the case, then you need to invite the angels into your life and ask them to play with you. Ask them to help you lighten up so you can enjoy life, even if it's for a small amount of time, in the midst of all your responsibilities.

Life is too short, and most people only discover this when they go through a serious illness or they've lost a loved one. Don't wait for this to happen to you. Give yourself permission to enjoy life and ask your angels to show you the opportunities to do this. Then pay attention. When you're invited to parties, to the theater, or any other fun activity, say yes and give yourself permission to have some fun. If you need the funds to support the things you love to do, then ask the angels for the extra money you need and trust that it will come.

Here are some different ways the angels might nudge you to play:

* Take a holiday. Ask the angels to help you find the time to go and the finances to support it. Make your plans and trust that you deserve a vacation.
* Forget the diet and enjoy your favourite ice cream or dessert.
* Take a spontaneous day and give yourself permission to do all the things you love.
* Start a hobby or take a class that you are interested in.
* Get on the floor and play with your children or grandchildren.
* Go to the cinema with friends or by yourself.
* Take a walk on the beach, build a sandcastle, or read your favourite book.
* Do nothing. Stop thinking you have to do something.

Believe that the angels want you to be happy and they will support you with everything you need to enjoy life. Your job is to feel worthy and deserving of receiving joy and taking the time to experience it. The next time you get an idea to have some fun or an opportunity comes your way, see it as a gift from your angels. Say yes and have some fun.

Angel Prayer

Prayer to lighten up: "Dearest angels, help me and remind me to accept joy, play, and fun into my life. Show me the opportunities and encourage me to take the time so I can enjoy life and live it to its fullest."

Parking Angels

Yes, there really are parking angels and you might not believe it until you try it out for yourself. The next time you're looking for a parking spot, call on the parking angels and ask them for the perfect spot closest to the entrance. Don't be surprised if it's either waiting for you or someone pulls out right when you get there. Just remember, it's always a kind gesture to thank your angels after receiving your perfect spot.

Calling on the parking angels is also a great way to get kids involved in asking for help from the angels. They think it's magical when the perfect spot reveals itself and it helps them believe that the angels are really listening. Sometimes with children you need to start with the small prayers so they feel more comfortable when it's time to ask for the bigger things in life. Once they witness the miracles of asking and receiving, they are more open to the possibilities of working with the angels.

Weather Angels

Reflect on this for a moment: You've worked really hard and it's time for a holiday and it's important for you to have nice weather to experience it to its fullest. Wouldn't it be nice if you could call on the help of the weather angels so you could really enjoy your holiday? It might be hard to believe that the angels can help you with the weather, but why wouldn't they want to help you experience a fun and enjoyable holiday?

So the next time you go on holiday or when you're having an important event like a party, graduation, or barbecue, pray to the weather angels beforehand and ask them for a beautiful, clear, and sunny day (if that's important) so everyone can fully enjoy the event. You can also call on the weather angels when you desire clear weather for traveling of any kind. Simply ask, "Please, weather angels, clear the way for smooth traveling and clear weather so we can reach our destination safely with ease and timeliness."

You can also call on the weather angels if you need help during unexpected weather conditions like heavy downpours or thunderstorms. For example, "Angels, please provide protection for myself and my loved ones and help us to feel safe as the effects of Mother Nature move peacefully through our surroundings."

Traveling Angels

Traveling can be very joyful, adventurous, and exciting, and other times it can be a journey into the unknown, where you experience fear, anxiety, and stress. Inviting the angels to travel with you can give you a sense of peace that you are not alone and you are being watched over, no matter what the situation might be.

There are many ways in which the angels can assist you while traveling:

⭑ When flying, request that the angels watch over the plane and the pilot and ask that your flight be safe, smooth, and on time. You can also imagine angels resting on the wings of the plane.

⭑ When traveling by car, ask the angels to watch over and protect your vehicle and all passengers with you. Ask for a clear path ahead so your travels are smooth and timely.

⭑ When traveling with luggage, ask your angels to watch over it and request that it arrive at your destination when you do.

⭑ When visiting unfamiliar places, ask for protection so you can feel safe and ask the angels to send the perfect people to help and guide you to the best places to visit, stay, and eat.

⭑ If you are traveling on business, ask the angels for everything you need to make it a pleasurable and successful trip.

⭑ Remember to ask for the weather you need to get to your destination and to enjoy it while you are there.

⭑ If loved ones are traveling without you, ask for the angels to protect them and watch over them until they return safely.

⭑ Ask the angels to watch over your home, your job or business, or any loved ones left behind while you are traveling.

★ If an issue or glitch in your travel plans emerges, ask the angels
   to resolve it quickly and to provide everything you need to
   work through it with ease and grace.

It is a gift to travel so you can connect with loved ones,
experience new places, create success in business, or to just rest
and relax. The angels want you to experience these opportunities
with ease and joy. So call on them and discover how they can
lighten the load for you when it comes to travel.

Shopping Angels

Those of you who love to shop might have a smile on your face
right now, imagining all these angels surrounding you with
shopping bags. If you really dislike shopping and you always have a
hard time picking out the perfect gift for your loved one, then keep
reading; there is heavenly help on its way. The shopping angels can
save you money and ease your life. For example:

★ Before going shopping, sit quietly and ask the angels to tell you
   the store where you can find what you need at the best price.
★ When shopping for someone else, ask their guardian angels to
   direct you to the perfect gift at the perfect price.
★ When you're overwhelmed with a big store or too much
   merchandise, ask the angels to guide you in the direction and
   show you exactly where you need to go.
★ Share with the angels how much money you have to spend.
   Ask them to help you spend it wisely and to guide you toward
   the perfect purchase.

☆ Check in with the angels before you make a purchase (especially if it's a major one or if you are a compulsive shopper) and notice how it feels. If you feel peaceful or warm, then it's right. If it doesn't feel right and you feel anxious or uncomfortable, then they are asking you to wait or they're trying to tell you that something better is coming.

Calling on your shopping angels can be very helpful. It can save you time and money. You don't need to go to a fancy department store to get a personal shopper because you have them all around you. Just call out and be specific about what you need and how you want them to help you. Then enjoy and have fun playing with your shopping angels!

Protect, Heal and Forgive with the Angels

Protection for Your Family

O ne of the most common fears people struggle with is the fear of losing someone they love. When panic sets in, the mind's imagination takes off just like a small snowball being pushed off the top of the hill and turning into a giant snowball. For example, a family member is late coming home from work, and your mind jumps to the assumption that they have been injured in a car accident. Or your child didn't call when they got to their friend's house, and your mind concludes that they've been abducted.

Angel Advice

Remember, there is no limit to the number of angels you can call on for help. Call on 10,000 angels for protection if you feel you need them. They are waiting in multitudes ready to assist you in any way they can.

☆ ☆ ☆ ☆ ☆ ☆ ☆ ☆ ☆ ☆ ☆ ☆ ☆ ☆ ☆

When fear begins to consume you, stop and call upon the angels of protection to help you and your loved ones. Immediately ask everyone's guardian angels to surround all those involved in love and protection. Choose to have faith and imagine them being embraced in the wings of the angels. Ask the angels to release your fear and replace it with peace. Remind yourself to stay present in the moment where everything is okay. Realise that your imagination has taken over and that fear is creating all the what ifs.

Call on the angels of protection in the following situations:

✶ When your loved one is late in coming home.
✶ When a loved one is sick or not feeling well.
✶ When your children are home alone and you're worried.
✶ When your loved one is going through a challenging time and you can't be with him.
✶ When your loved one is going through emotional issues and you don't know what to do.
✶ When your loved one is traveling alone and you're worried for her safety.

In all of these situations you can call on the angels to watch over your loved ones. Recognise that your thoughts wander into the what ifs and acknowledge that you're worried and afraid. Seize the opportunity to shift your thoughts from fear into faith. Ask the angels for help and know that everyone involved will benefit when you shift your intention from fear to love.

Protection for Your Home

Your home is your sacred dwelling place. You want your home to be filled with a positive, loving, and peaceful energy. When your home is filled with love, it feels light and happy and everyone feels comfortable and safe. If there is negativity in the home, you might feel heaviness in the air or you may feel uncomfortable being in the house. When this happens, call on the angels of protection and ask them to clear the energy in your home. Request that they remove all negativity so it feels peaceful once again.

Fear can easily set in when you're home alone and your mind wanders to that scary film or that dreadful story from the news. What if you could feel more peace when you're home alone? What if you could trust that your children or pets were being watched over when you're not at home? Imagine how good you would feel if you knew there was someone watching over your home twenty-four hours a day while you were on holiday. Whenever you are faced with any of these situations, call on the angels to watch over your home and ask them to keep it safe from harm. These divine helpers protect your home so you can have peace and enjoy life, feeling safe wherever you are.

Asking for Healing

Healing can take place on many levels and the angels can help you with all aspects of healing. The first step you need to take in order to initiate your healing process is to simply ask, "Angels, help me heal." Then be specific. Ask for the help you need and share with the angels how you want to feel when you are restored to full health and wholeness. Try these examples of asking the angels for help with healing:

✴ You are in physical pain. Ask the angels to ease your pain and ask them to guide you to the resources you need (rest, doctors, healers, or medicine) in order to heal quickly and completely.

✴ You are emotionally depressed. Ask the angels for peace and the help you need to heal the source of your emotional pain.

✴ You are struggling with relationship issues. Ask the angels for healing so all involved experience harmony, peace, and cooperation.

✴ You are mentally confused and forgetful. Ask the angels for clarity so you can remember.

Angel Prayer

A prayer to invoke healing: "Dearest angels of healing, please give me everything I need to heal completely. I am willing to heal on every level—mind, body, and spirit. I surrender and trust that you know exactly what I need and you will show me the way. I am paying attention and I commit to taking action on anything I must do in order to achieve wholeness."

After you ask the angels for help and you're specific about what you want, then you need to surrender and trust. The angels know how to help you heal as a whole person in mind, body, and spirit. This is important because it's not unusual that in order for someone to heal physically they need to heal emotionally. So remember, when you ask the angels for healing, be willing to surrender and trust that you will be given exactly what you need in order to accomplish this.

The last step when asking the angels for help is your responsibility. Pay attention and take action on anything you receive intuitively or from outside resources. For example, let's say you've asked the angels to heal your depression and someone tells you about a meditation class. It's your job to pay attention and take action, knowing that your angels have sent you an opportunity to heal.

These are the steps you take to begin and complete your healing process:

1. Ask for healing.
2. Be specific about what you want to feel.
3. Surrender and trust the angels.
4. Pay attention and take action.
5. Say thank you for the healing.

Physical Healing

Your natural state of being is one of health and vitality. Do you remember the last time you were feeling sick and you had the flu or a cold? Now recall how good it felt and how grateful you were when you finally recovered.

Your body can be a wonderful messenger. If you are out of balance physically, mentally, or emotionally, disease will come knocking at your door trying to get your attention. Your body is telling you it's time to heal and take care of yourself. The angels of healing can help you do this and they want to assist you in bringing your body back into balance.

Whenever you're in pain or you're suffering from illness, call out to the angels and ask them for physical healing. If you are in pain, ask them to relieve your pain so you can feel more peaceful. When you are sick or suffering from illness, ask them to give you everything you need so you can return to your natural state of health and well-being. Your job is to take responsibility for your health and follow your inner guidance so you can do what's necessary to heal yourself.

The angels of healing can help if you:

★ Ask for the best medical care for your highest and greatest good.

★ Ask for the patience you need to rest and heal.

★ Ask for the emotional and mental healing you need to physically get better.

★ Ask for the earth angels who can help you and be willing to accept their help.

★ Ask for any holistic or alternative approaches that will help you heal.

★ Ask for any financial support you need to fund your healing process.

★ Ask for a miracle.

The angels of healing can provide you with the support and resources you need to accelerate your healing process. When you are out of balance, surrender and trust that all is well. Your body and the angels are helping you remember that it's time to take care of yourself.

Emotional Healing

Most people don't realise this, but your emotional well-being is just as important as your physical health; they are interrelated. When you are peaceful and content with your life, your body feels light, you take care of yourself, and you stay healthy. When you feel unfulfilled, depressed, and confused about your life, your body feels heavy, you don't take care of yourself, and you experience more sickness.

Throughout your life you will have many experiences, and emotional highs and emotional lows. Your health depends on how you process your emotions. Ask yourself, "Do I process my emotions in a healthy way or do I bury them within?"

Angel Advice

The best thing you can do when you're feeling your emotions bubbling to the surface is BREATHE! Remember this simple saying: "Feel it to heal it." Next time, instead of blocking your emotions, let yourself feel and just breathe. This is where healing takes place.

The angels of emotional healing can help you release and heal any toxic emotions that are affecting your life in a negative way. This can free you so you can experience more peace, joy, happiness, health, and overall well-being. The angels of emotional healing can help you. Here's how you can ask for help:

☆ When you notice painful emotions like sadness, anger, resentment, or hurt bubbling to the surface, call on the angels and ask for healing.

☆ Sit with the angels in prayer or meditation and ask them to help you heal. Share with them how you feel in the moment (you can always write about it) and then tell them how you want to feel.

☆ If you feel you need counseling or support of some kind, ask the angels to guide you to what you require in order to heal.

☆ Ask the angels to guide you to the perfect books, classes, or anything else that can bring you healing or new awareness.

☆ Before bed, ask the angels to help you heal during your dream state.

⋆ Ask for a miracle and a feeling of inner peace.

Healing for the Dying and Grieving

There are countless angel stories where the dying and their family members describe the presence of angels or a visitation from a loved one. They come to the dying and their family members in hopes of reassuring them that they are being helped from the other side. Imagine the comfort you would feel if you knew the angels were by your side helping you or your loved ones transition from this world into the next.

If you have a loved one who is dying, call on the angels for help. Their job is to comfort the dying and to help them when they're ready to cross over into heaven. Once they're in heaven they will stay with them, helping them make the transition as they adjust to their new surroundings. Be reassured that they will make sure that there is no suffering at the time of death, whether it's a sudden death or the person has been sick. They will also lend their support and provide healing for the grieving family members. Call on the angels if you are grieving a loss of any kind and ask them to help you heal. Know that they will stay by your side until you transition through your loss and you feel peace again.

How Do You Forgive?

Forgiveness means letting go of any resentment, hurt, and anger you may feel because of the actions or choices of another. Self-forgiveness means letting go of any guilt or resentment you may feel toward yourself because of the choices you've made in the past.

☆ ☆ ☆ ☆ ☆ ☆ ☆ ☆ ☆ ☆ ☆ ☆ ☆ ☆ ☆

If you really think about it, you've probably had many experiences where you've had the opportunity to practice forgiveness both for yourself and others.

When you are unable to forgive the emotions consume you. The angels of forgiveness can help heal these emotions that bind you to the past. They will provide you with everything you need to transform your painful emotions and ultimately come to a place of forgiveness.

Steps to Forgiveness

The angels are waiting to help you. Use the following steps if you are ready to forgive another or if it's time to forgive yourself:

1. Acknowledge you are suffering from not being able to forgive.
2. Declare to the angels and yourself that you are willing to forgive.
3. Tell your angels how you want to feel and what you want to experience on the other side of forgiveness (remember, you do not have to figure out how it's going to happen).
4. Ask the angels to help you let go, heal, and forgive.
5. Pay attention to your emotions, your dreams, and any guidance you receive that will help you reach forgiveness.
6. Ask the angels to help you be patient and persistent until you reach a place of compassion, understanding, and peace.

As you take these steps toward healing, be patient with yourself and trust the angels are working with you. They know how hard it is to forgive when you've been hurt by another, especially if it's someone you've loved or trusted. You will know when you've reached true forgiveness because you will no longer feel resentment, anger, or revenge. You will experience a feeling of acceptance and an inner peace; then you can move forward. You will no longer be triggered by the hurt from your past and you might even feel compassion for the one who has hurt you.

Ask the Angel

What if I have a hard time forgiving someone?

Remember that forgiveness is about you and your desire to free yourself from any past pain. Go into meditation and ask the angels to help you understand why those who hurt you made the choices they did. If all else fails, surrender daily and ask them to lead you to forgiveness.

Self-Forgiveness

When you're unwilling to forgive yourself for something you did in your past, you hold onto toxic emotions: resentment, guilt, and feelings of unworthiness. The angels can help you, even if you don't know how to forgive yourself.

Take the following steps with the angels to heal through forgiveness:

1. Acknowledge your feelings of remorse and the mistakes you've made.
2. Declare to the angels that you are willing to heal and forgive yourself.
3. Contact someone you feel you need to make amends with. (Be cautious. If you feel it would cause more pain and hurt, then don't do it, just heal with the angels.)
4. Admit and accept your mistakes. Have compassion for yourself.
5. Learn from your mistakes and use them as knowledge for your future.
6. Ask the angels to help you heal and forgive yourself completely so you can experience inner peace.

The angels of healing and forgiveness can help you become one with self-love and acceptance. They know it does not serve you or anyone else involved when you choose not to forgive yourself. So open your heart and be willing to heal and forgive yourself. You will discover that as you do this, your heart will expand with the feelings of peace, compassion, and loving kindness.

Meditation for Forgiveness

Use the following meditation when you need help with forgiveness. Call on the angels of forgiveness and set your intention that you are open and willing for healing to take place. Ask for a full healing to take place so you can forgive and move forward to peace, compassion, and understanding.

☆　☆　☆　☆　☆　☆　☆　☆　☆　☆　☆　☆　☆　☆　☆

Find a quiet and comfortable place where no one will bother you. Put on some nice, soothing music in the background and set your intention. If you choose, you can write to your angels beforehand, expressing your feelings and requesting the help you need.

Now take a deep breath and close your eyes. Ask the healing angels to surround you in a beautiful circle of love, healing, and protection. (Pause) Affirm to them, "I am open and willing to experience a full healing and to forgive myself and everyone involved. (Pause) Angels of forgiveness, give me everything I need to become one with this prayer.

Now imagine yourself being surrounded in a green emerald healing light that brings healing and protection. (Pause) See a chair or a couple of chairs being placed in front of you. It's time to initiate forgiveness. It is important to remember you do not have to forgive the act that has been done, you just need to free yourself from any pain it's caused you.

Call forth anyone whom you need to forgive and ask them to sit in the chair in front of you. If you do not feel safe, ask the angels to protect you so no harm can come to you. Then say to that person, "I am choosing to forgive you so I can free myself from any pain that you've caused me. (Pause) What you did to me hurt me and it's not okay. (Pause) Yet, it's time for me to heal, and in order to do that, I need to forgive you. (Pause) I am ready to send you healing so you can choose to act in a positive way in the future. (Pause)

Imagine the angels of healing and forgiveness surrounding the other person with a light of compassion and healing. (Pause) Hand them a symbolic rose that signifies your willingness to forgive and shows that you are choosing to practice compassion. (Pause) Then release them completely and ask the angels to complete the healing between you. Affirm, "I am free. You are free. I release you. I release me. I forgive you. I forgive me." (Pause)

Now ask the angels to heal your heart, mind, body, and spirit so you are freed and healed of any past emotions that hold you back from full forgiveness. (Pause) Imagine the angels filling your heart with a radiant pink light symbolising love and compassion. (Pause) Then imagine every cell and thought being illuminated in this beautiful healing pink light. (Pause)

Close the meditation affirming, "I am free. I forgive myself and _____ (state the names of anyone you forgave). We are all free to move forward in healing, compassion, and love.

Angels of forgiveness, please help me move forward with the gifts and lessons from this experience and help me remember the wisdom learned. Thank you for this healing, the gifts of forgiveness, and your loving assistance."

Take some nice deep breaths and imagine yourself illuminated in the pink light. Breathe in gratitude and the peace you feel. Ask the angels to continue to guide you and embrace you in their love. Slowly and gently come back into the present moment knowing it's a new beginning.

ENHANCING YOUR RELATIONSHIPS AND CAREER WITH THE ANGELS

How the Angels Can Help with Relationships

Relationships can be joyous, but they can also be complicated; this is why the angels assist you on your journey down the path of love and relationships. To live in harmony and cooperation you must be willing to ask for the help you need.

A beautiful quote by Ella Wheeler Wilcox is,
"There is only one happiness in life: to love and be loved."

Here are some ways the angels can help you enhance your relationships:

★ Ask the angels for help when you feel disconnected from someone you love or admire. Ask for healing to take place so you can feel reconnected and close once again.

★ Ask the angels for help when anger or resentment exists in relationships.

★ Ask that everyone involved experience peace through healing and forgiveness.

★ Ask the angels for help if you would like new loving friendships to come into your life.

★ Ask the angels for help if you want to meet your soul mate.

★ Ask the angels for help if you would like more romance and passion in your marriage.

★ Ask the angels to help you heal from a divorce or separation.

* Ask the angels for any help you need to have a loving relationship with your children.
* Ask the angels to help you with clear and honest communication.

These are just some of the ways the angels can help you when you choose to heal your relationships or experience more love. Whatever the situation is, know the angels are waiting in unconditional love to assist you.

Enhancing Your Relationships with Family

What if someone told you that you chose each and every one of your family members before you birthed into this lifetime? There is a divine plan and the family dynamics you chose and continue to take part in were all designed for your soul to grow and evolve. No matter if you believe this or not, throughout your lifetime you will experience great joy and heartache when it comes to family. The angels were gifted to you so you could reach out and ask for their help, especially when it relates to family.

Take a moment and reflect. Are you feeling any stress, tension, or disharmony between yourself and any family members? If so, the angels encourage you to surrender your relationships for healing. They know exactly what needs to take place in order for peace to occur. After you surrender your relationship issue to the angels, be open to their loving guidance so miracles can happen. They may ask you to practice forgiveness or they may direct you to step into the other person's shoes and see the situation from a different perspective. Don't be surprised if the phone rings and the person you have been in conflict with makes amends with you.

Creating Cooperative and Harmonious Relationships

Outside of family, you have many other relationships that affect your day and your life in both positive and sometimes challenging ways. This can involve friends, neighbours, co-workers, customers, and even strangers. Life seems to be in the flow when you attract people into your life who are positive and cooperative. However, the road can get bumpy and the day can seem long when you encounter people who are challenging and who push your buttons.

First of all, ask the angels of relationships to send more people into your life who are positive, joyful, and cooperative. Then ask the angels to gently remove those people from your life who drain your energy and no longer serve your highest and best. Give the angels some time to manifest this prayer and then see if there are still people left in your life who are challenging. Trust that they are still around because you have more healing to do and there are lessons to be learned. Your soul has called them forth in order for you to evolve and grow. When this happens, ask the angels of relationships to help you learn the soul lesson needed in order to heal. Then pray for peace and harmony to coexist in the relationship.

Angel Prayer

Prayer for Harmonious Relationships

Help me attract loving and supportive people with positive attitudes into my life. Help me let go or release me from any relationships that are unhealthy and not serving my highest and best. If there are lessons to learn from difficult relationships, help me learn them quickly so I may heal and the relationship can transform into a peaceful and harmonious experience. Thank you, angels, for your loving help and support.

Healing with the Angels
After a Breakup or Divorce

Healing and grieving from a loss in a relationship is hard for everyone involved. There is a tremendous amount of emotion that one has to deal with after a breakup or a divorce: sadness, confusion, depression, anger, grief, and aloneness. The angels want to step in and assist you in as many ways as they can during these challenging and emotional times. Even though these times may be difficult, with the angels' help you can get through it more quickly and you can emerge from it with more strength, healing, wisdom, and empowerment. There are different ways the angels can help you after a breakup or divorce:

✳ Ask the angels to help you heal your heart and all those affected by the breakup.

✳ Ask the angels to help everyone involved with forgiveness so you can all move on and be free.

✳ Ask the angels for the resources you need after the breakup—money, housing, insurance, etc.

✳ Ask the angels to help you heal your emotions so you can find peace again.

✳ Ask the angels for clarity and wisdom so you can grow and accept the gifts and lessons learned from the relationship.

✳ Ask the angels to open your heart again so you can love and be loved.

The angels want to help you transition through loss and grief so you can take your power back and move forward in independence, joy, happiness, and freedom to love again. Ask for the help you need and realize you do not have to go through it alone. There is a team of divine helpers ready to carry you when you need it and give you the courage to walk in strength and independence.

Meditation to Create Harmonious Relationships

You can use this meditation to create harmonious relationships wherever you need it in your life: with family, coworkers, friends, past relationships, and even new people you meet.

Go to your sacred space where you can be alone with the angels. Call on your team of divine helpers. Ask them to support you in fulfilling your heart's desires. Relax and breathe with the loving energy that surrounds you. Know that you are not alone and you are very loved. (Pause)

Now, set your intention with the angels: "My desire is to create peaceful and harmonious relationships with _____ (state their names). (Pause) Dearest angels, help us break down any walls of fear so we come together in understanding, compassion, and love."

With your eyes closed, call forth the person or persons you wish to create harmony with in your life. Now imagine the walls of fear coming down between all involved, including you. (Pause)

Now feel or see love flowing back and forth from each person's heart. (Pause) Ask the angels to heal all involved and to initiate peace and harmony back into your lives. (Pause)

Move forward into the future and see the relationship peacefully resolved. (Pause) Imagine and feel everyone living in harmony and cooperation. (Pause) Feel gratitude and thank everyone involved, including the angels. When you're ready, slowly and gently come back into the present moment and trust that all is well.

Witness how this meditation creates change, which brings peace. Open your heart to the healing and miracles coming your way.

Trust that the angels are working with all involved and your job is to believe that anything is possible with the help of the angels.

Finding Your Soul Mate

The angels will help you find the love of your life when you ask them for assistance. They wish for you all the experiences of love and communion that can only take place when two souls come together in partnership.

The first step is to sit with your angels and make a wish list of your desires and what you want to feel and experience in your partnership. If you have had previous experiences with other relationships, then you have more wisdom and knowledge to clarify what you do want and what you don't want. When making your list, only affirm and list what you do want to experience, the positive not the negative.

Here are some ideas when creating your wish list to the angels:

☆ What does your soul mate look like? Examples: handsome, athletic, tall, short, dark or light hair, nice eyes, great dresser.

☆ What does it feel like when you are with him? Examples: warm, connected, happy, fulfilled, spontaneous, comfortable, genuine, fun.

☆ What are the characteristics of your soul mate and your relationship? Examples: committed, trusting, honest and open communication, supportive, fun, passionate.

☆ What's important to you? Examples: someone spiritual, likes to travel, likes to work out, loves good food, good with kids, supportive of your career, likes to have a good time, conversational, good around the house.

☆ What is your life like after you get together? Examples: we have financial security and abundance, we spend quality time together, we are passionate, we easily communicate, we appreciate each other, we laugh together.

Angel Advice

Spend some time in your sacred space when you create your wishlist. Be specific and only state the positive. If you choose, you may review it with a friend. She might have suggestions for additions to your list.

Your list is going to be very individual to who you are and what you like. Be honest and specific with the angels. Create your wish list and then surrender it to your angels. They will work diligently behind the scenes to bring you together at the perfect time and in the perfect place. Your job is to believe, affirm, and visualise your soul mate in your meditation and imagine your wish list coming true.

Meditation for Connecting You with Your Soul Mate

This is a powerful meditation that works to help you connect and meet your soul mate. Get ready for miracles if you choose to invite them into your life.

Find a quiet place to sit and bring your soul mate wish list with you. If you choose, you can put some quiet music, in the background, get comfortable, and place your wish list on your lap. Take some nice deep breaths and set your intention that you are going to work with the angels to connect with your soul mate.

Call in your guardian angels and your soul mate's guardian angels and ask Archangel Chamuel and Archangel Haniel to join you. Ask them to create a beautiful circle of divine light, love, and power around you. Breathe in and believe they are going to help you become one with your true love on a soul level and on a physical level. (Pause)

Now imagine your soul as a star in the sky. Now send a call out to your soul mate. There are many stars in the sky, but one seems to shine very bright and it twinkles more than the others. Look for it or feel it—it's there! (Pause)

Now see that star coming toward your star until they merge and become one big, brilliant, bright star. (Pause) Now ask your soul and your angels to call out to your physical beings on the earth plane. Imagine you are both stars on the earth and you attract each other until you finally merge on the earth plane. Just like the two stars came together on the soul plane, they come together on the earth plane. See or feel that happening. (Pause) Through the help of the angels you easily find each other, you are drawn to each other, and you are destined to be together.

Now imagine, or pretend if you need to, that you are living together in happiness, commitment, joy, peace, and harmony. Imagine and feel it in every cell of your being. (Pause) Thank your soul and your angels for bringing you together and for the miracles of your love. (Pause)

Feel the gratitude and then slowly breathe back into the moment, holding on to your vision and the feeling of true love.

Help with Your Career

Think about how much time you spend at your job daily, weekly, and yearly. Then add to that the amount of time you spend after work just thinking about your job. When you add it all up, you spend a great deal of time on the job. If you're content with your job it can be rewarding, but if you're unhappy, the days can seem very long. The angels want to help you spend this valuable time in the most fulfilling way. Here are some different ways the angels can help you in your career:

✶ Ask the angels to help you experience harmonious and cooperative relationships at work.

✶ Ask the angels to help you when negotiating compensation (hint . . . ask for better than you could ever imagine).

✶ Ask the angels for a positive attitude so you can recognize the blessings during your day.

✶ Ask the angels to help you with balance between work, family, and play.

✶ Ask the angels to help you create a new business or be inspired with new ideas.

✶ Ask the angels for confidence when speaking with others or presenting your ideas.

★ Ask the angels to release you from any stress and provide you with peace and ease.

These are just some of the ways the angels can assist you in your career. If there is something specific going on and you would like the angels' help, then sit with them in meditation or pray with them in your car before you go to work. Share with them what you would like to feel once everything is resolved and then trust that they will do everything they can to assist you. Remember, you are not alone on the job. The angels can be your team in spirit, helping you every step of the way.

Angel Prayer

Prayer for Help with Your Career

Angels, I invite you into my life and I ask for your loving assistance. I would like help with the following situation (state the circumstances and what you desire). My wish is to experience (state the feeling outcome you desire) when this is all resolved. I know you will help me and I will stay open to your guidance. I expect a miraculous resolution and an outcome better than I could ever imagine. Thank you, angels.

Finding a New Job

Are you looking for a new job or career? The angels are eager to help and they want you to have a fulfilling job where you can experience happiness, pride, joy, and even take home a rewarding pay. They know you deserve the best and now it's time for you to expect it and accept it.

The first step to take with the angels is to sit down and create a wish list of what you want to experience in your ideal job. Get clear about what you want and what you don't want and then state on your wish list only your true desires.

Here are some questions to ask yourself while creating your list:

★ What are you passionate about? What do you love to do? Examples: I love to work with people. I love to be creative. I love working with numbers. I love helping other people. I love creative solutions.

★ What is your schedule of hours and days you work?

★ What are the people like with whom you interact or do you work independently? Examples: cooperative, fun, lighthearted, hard workers, successful, team players.

★ How far away is your work or do you work at home?

★ How do you feel when you're working at your new job? Examples: happy to go to work, productive, creative, enthusiastic, grateful, easy, content.

★ How much are you getting paid or how much are you making? What are your benefits?

★ How does it benefit your personal life? Examples: I come home happy from work. I have balance between my work, family, and play. I have more than enough time and money to go on vacation. My family is well provided for.

Now, take all your desires and create a positive affirmation for each intention. Write it with feeling and emotion and state it in the present tense as if it was happening right now. For example, "I am so grateful I am working with people who are supportive, enthusiastic, and helpful. Everyone enjoys their job and we are well taken care of by the company."

After you create your list, call on the angels of career and purpose and share with them your list of desires. Then surrender your wish list to the angels and trust that they will do everything in their power to help you create what you want. Your job is to hold the vision of your perfect job and believe it's possible and already done. Remember to stay open and pay attention to the signs and synchronicities and also your dreams and intuition. The angels will use all of these forms of communication to lead you to the perfect job.

Additional Resources

Angel Cards

Angel Therapy Oracle Cards by Doreen Virtue
Archangel Oracle Cards by Doreen Virtue
Angel Blessings by Kimberly Marooney
Daily Guidance from Your Angels Oracle Cards by Doreen Virtue
Messages from Your Angels by Doreen Virtue
Healing with the Angel Oracle Cards by Doreen Virtue

Guided Meditation CDs

Angel Attunement by Karen Paolino
Chakra Workout Meditations by Elizabeth Harper
Spark the Light by Karen Paolino

Meditation Music

Liquid Mind CD series
Steven Halpern's Inner Peace Music

GLOSSARY

Abundance
Having more than an adequate quantity or supply; an overflowing fullness and great plenty.

Affirmation
Declaring the truth through a positive statement.

Alchemy
A power or process of transforming something common into something special.

Angel cards
A deck of cards used for doing angel readings. The cards have various illustrations of the angels and they each have a message of divine guidance.

Angel reading
A method of divination where you connect to the angels to receive messages of divine guidance about all aspects of your life.

Angelic realm
A spiritual realm of pure love where the angels reside.

Angels
Messengers of love who serve as guardians and helpers between heaven and earth.

Apparition
When an angelic being or a deceased loved one becomes visible and you can see them with your eyes open.

Archangels
A higher order of angels that oversee the angels. They have the ability to be with everyone simultaneously.

Ascended masters
Divine helpers. These beings of light walked before you on this earth and during their lifetimes they were great teachers. They have now ascended into heaven and their role is to help all those that need them.

Ascension
When in reference to Christ, it means the rising of his body into heaven. In New Age terms, it means transforming your energy from a lower vibration into a higher vibration.

Attunement
To adjust or harmonize your vibration with the angels.

Beliefs
A mental acceptance or conviction

that something is true.

Chakras
The seven spiritual energy centers of the body.

Chanting
To recite something in a repetitive tone or to make melodic sounds with your voice.

Clairaudience
Clear hearing. This is when you experience or hear clear thoughts or words flowing through your mind and no one is physically there talking to you.

Claircognizance
Clear knowing. When you have an inner knowing you feel very strong that something is true or you know beyond any doubt that you need to take action.

Clairgustance
Clear taste. When you experience this, you have a clear taste of something in your mouth without any explanation of why it's happening.

Clairolfactory
Clear smell. When you use this ability, you can smell something even though it's not physically in your presence.

Clairsentience
Clear feeling. This is when you receive information as a feeling in your body.

Clairvoyance
Clear vision. This is when you have visions, images, or symbols presented to you through your inner vision.

Coincidence
When two things happen at the same time for no apparent reason.

Discernment
To gain insight or understanding about something that might have been confusing.

Divine guidance
Receiving clarity, direction, or inspiration from a divine source.

Divine inspiration
When you are guided or motivated by the divine to take action and express the inspiration.

Divine intervention
When the angels intervene and perform a miracle.

Divine magic
A magical occurrence as a result of divine intervention.

Divine resolution
When a problem or an issue is

resolved miraculously by the divine.

Earthbound spirits
Deceased humans who are hanging around the earth plane. Some people refer to them as ghosts.

Ego
The part of your personality self that sees itself separate from the angels. It usually wants to be in control and it focuses on fear.

Energy
An immeasurable universal source and power.

Faith
A firm belief or trust in something for which there is no proof.

Guardian angels
Your personal angels. Everyone has at least two guardian angels who were gifted to you by God.

Guided meditation
A meditation that is guided by the voice of the facilitator.

Heaven on Earth
Having all the experiences of heaven here on Earth: bliss, unity, abundance, miracles, wholeness, joy, peace, and unconditional love.

Hierarchy
An order of holy beings organized in a successive ranking order of power.

Intention
Focusing your thoughts and feelings on what you desire to create and experience with determination.

Intuition
The instinctual knowing you get when you listen to your inner senses.

Invocation
Asking for help or support from the angels.

Law of attraction
When your focused thoughts, feelings, and emotions are charged with energy or vibration and it acts as a magnet that attracts into your life exactly what you're focused on.

Life purpose
When you've found a way to express yourself and it feels meaningful and significant to you. It's fulfilling and you feel passionate about it.

Manifestation
A materialized form that was created from a thought or a prayer.

Meditation
To engage in reflection, prayer, or contemplation.

Medium
Someone who communicates with deceased loved ones to deliver messages of healing and love.

Miracle
An extraordinary event manifesting divine intervention into human affairs or an extremely outstanding or unusual event, thing, or accomplishment.

Nature angels
The angels of Mother Nature; the fairies.

Near-death experience
When someone is close to death or they are pronounced clinically dead and they have an experience of life after death.

Precognition
When you receive visions or information about a future event.

Prosperity
Being successful and flourishing and thriving in financial respects.

Quantum physics
A science that deals with the effects of invisible energy. It studies the fundamental nature of the universe and it describes the universe as very different from the world we see.

Sacred space
A place of retreat where you can step away from the busyness of your everyday life and experience peace and relaxation.

Sign
A confirmation from your angels.

Spiritual toolbox
A place in your mind where you hold all your spiritual teachings.

Spirituality
Your personal and private relationship and connection with the divine.

Synchronicity
A coincidental occurrence of two or more events that have no relevance to one another, yet when it takes place, it has great meaning to the person who is witnessing or experiencing it.

Third eye
The spiritual eye that receives intuitive information and spiritual visions. This energy center is located behind the forehead between the eyes.

Vibration
A characteristic emanation, aura, or spirit that infuses or vitalizes

someone or something and that can be instinctively sensed or experienced.

Wish list
A list of desires and intentions you would like to manifest into physical

Index

☆　☆　☆　☆　☆　☆　☆　☆　☆　☆　☆　☆　☆　☆　☆